"Full of food and mu ... *[genda* is a collection of brief ill ... ke a good friend with a story to ... k Bailey is a writer who wants to ... is one of discoveries, small mar ... celebrations."

  —MATTHEW OLZMANN, author of *Contradictions in Design*

"Knowledgeable, funny, and utterly curious, Bailey comes off as everyone's favorite uncle, who returns from far-flung reaches to share wise tales and good wine. And though this book teems with quirky asides, curious tangents, and plenty of self-deprecating humor, what comes through strongest is a decades-long romance that is worthy of study and emulation."

  —JOEY FRANKLIN, author of *My Wife Wants You to Know I'm Happily Married*

"Clearing out the parental home, finding the best gelato in an Italian village, using photos to purchase (sans language) a screwdriver in Shanghai: Rick Bailey's reminiscences are enhanced by research, literary references, and the simple pleasure he takes in the world around us. This is engaging, thoughtful work."

  —TERRY BLACKHAWK, Kresge Arts in Detroit Literary Fellow

"Hooray for miscellany, for odds and ends gathered between covers, designed to charm and surprise! Rick Bailey launches right into his quirky thoughts on myriad subjects (music, art, food, travel, health, language, etc.) and doesn't let up for the duration of this wonderfully original, unpredictable book. *The Enjoy Agenda* subtly and insistently suggests that life is a gift to be enjoyed, a goal the book itself fulfills for readers."

  —PATRICK MADDEN, author of *Quotidiana* and *Sublime Physick*

"In this startling new collection of mini-essays, Rick Bailey re-creates for us what Virginia Woolf calls *moments of being*, those bright bursts of beauty, loss, communion, and bewilderment that constitute a life. Here we have everything from a boy's first glimpse of the horror of an automobile accident to a grown man's regret that he cannot carry the burden of the anvil he has inherited from his father, brief meditations not only on wine and ragu, but dumplings, dancing, death, gelato, toothaches, ER scares, and the profound mystery of why Europeans can eat pastries for breakfast and still remain thin. I defy you to read one of these deliciously addictive essays without gulping down the entire book."

—EILEEN POLLACK, author of *The Only Woman in the Room*

"Rick Bailey's essays overflow with warmth, humor, truth. In this new collection, a woven memoir, we travel with him to Italy, China, and around his home state of Michigan. Bailey invites us to delight with him in food and music, in family and friends, in his zest for life, with all its twists and turns. *The Enjoy Agenda* offers keen observations, nuggets of wisdom, stories of the heart. Quoting from one of his essays—'Life is short. Don't forget to gelato.'—I add: Don't forget to read Rick Bailey.'"

—CHRISTINE RHEIN, poet and the author of *Wild Flight*

"It's not often I read a book of essays and fall in love with the writer and the characters in his life. But that's what happened reading Richard Bailey's *The Enjoy Agenda*, a collection of forty short essays. Bailey speaks to us like he's one of our best friends, commenting on everyday items like those old school pictures, jet lag, health changes as we age, where to find the best gelato, and dozens of other amusing topics. *The Enjoy Agenda* takes us through the stuff of one man's life journey, and, imaginatively, we all end up with 'a reminder of where we've been, where and who we come from; a reminder of who we loved and who loved us.' Read it and *enjoy*."

—DAVID JAMES, author of *My Torn Dance Card* and *She Dances Like Mussolini*

# THE ENJOY AGENDA

RICK BAILEY

# The Enjoy Agenda

## AT HOME AND ABROAD

University of Nebraska Press • LINCOLN

"Beheading" originally appeared in *First Stop Fiction;* "Idaho" originally appeared in *Pure Slush*, 2 (September 23, 2014). Excerpt from "Dirge Without Music" from *Collected Poems*. Copyright 1928, © 1955 by Edna St. Vincent Millay and Norma Millay Ellis, by permission of the Permissions company, Inc., on behalf of Holly Pepper, literary executor, the Millay Society. www.millay.org

Library of Congress Cataloging-in-Publication Data

Names: Bailey, Richard, 1952– author.

Title: The enjoy agenda: at home and abroad / Rick Bailey.

Description: Lincoln: University of Nebraska Press, 2019.

Identifiers: LCCN 2018036113

ISBN 9781496214690 (pbk.: alk. paper)

ISBN 9781496215246 (epub)

ISBN 9781496215253 (mobi)

ISBN 9781496215260 (pdf)

Subjects: LCSH: Bailey, Richard, 1952– | Older men—United States—Biography. | Baby boom generation—United States—Biography. | Popular culture—United States—Anecdotes. | Music fans—United States—Biography. | United States—Civilization—Anecdotes. | United States—Social life and customs—20th century—Anecdotes. | United States—Social life and customs—21st century—Anecdotes. | Bailey, Richard,—Travel. |Americans—Italy—Biography.

Classification: LCC CT275.B225 A3 2019 | DDC 305.26/10092

[B]—dc23 LC record available at https://lccn.loc.gov/2018036113

Set in Garamond Premier Pro by E. Cuddy.

For Tizi

# CONTENTS

# Inner Music

I TOOK A GUITAR with me to England in 1974. My wife never tires of reminding me. At an airport, whenever we see a guy lugging a bulky black guitar case down the concourse or cramming it into the overhead compartment (and taking up all the space), she points at me, shakes her head, and laughs.

"That was you," she whispers.

It was a course in Shakespeare in Stratford-upon-Avon. We were a group of thirty theater and literature students with a few senior citizens as well, one of whom had a slightly broken neck and needed to hang in traction every morning in the rooming house where we stayed. The group read *Richard II* and *King John* and *King Lear*, saw the plays performed, and motored around the Cotswolds in a big bus. Mostly we guzzled warm, dark, heavy beer in pubs and acquired English accents. "Lovely" became my favorite adjective. Lovely beer, lovely performance. Walking down to breakfast every day I'd see Jean dangling in the doorway of her room. "Good morning, Jean. Lovely day, isn't it?"

"Really," my wife says. "What were you thinking?"

I tell her I thought I needed to practice. Writers keep journals. Artists fill sketchbooks. Musicians practice. The rock band I was in would have gigs as soon as I got back. Wouldn't my licks get rusty in a few weeks?

The first few nights I was there, before dinner in our house I closed the door of my room, took out my instrument, and played for a few minutes, feeling mildly ridiculous. In the airport and on the bus to Stratford, wherever I carried my luggage and my guitar case, the theater students would all give me kind of an expectant look. Like, *Let's all sing!* I wouldn't have thought of playing the guitar *for* people, not for longer than a few minutes, anyway. I was not a campfire musician. I didn't know any show tunes. I'd been to too many parties where an ebullient (self-indulgent) guitarist hijacked the room, which I found unbearable.

THE OTHER DAY AT the gym I was invited to think about music, about the eminent strangeness of gratuitous music in particular. A woman on the treadmill next to me, plugged into her personal listening device, was emitting rhythmic, atonal subvocalizations (a.k.a. humming). I didn't want to listen. Who would want to listen? Maybe she didn't know she was doing it or she thought no one could hear. Maybe she was happy.

Humming, that annoying scratching of a musical itch, almost always seems out of place. The most famous hummer I know, pianist Glenn Gould, hums through his virtuoso performances of Bach, among them the *Goldberg Variations*. Along with that beautiful piano music you hear this growling sound, faint but unmistakable. Sean Malone, a musician who writes on music theory and music cognition, and is also an assistant professor of music at Carnegie Mellon, observes, "Gould may have visualized a large-scale, amodal image of the composition's structure—an abstract conception of themes, climaxes, and form, etc.—transcending the tactile and physical requirements of performing the piece." Malone might maintain that humming is the sound of premusic or metamusic. Maybe. To me it just sounds like antimusic.

When I was in still in the classroom, every so often I would have a student, usually older, usually female, who was excited about learning, deliriously happy to be in school. Often she would sit in the front row, right next to my desk. Early in the semester, before the honeymoon had ended (before I started giving critiques and grades), when asked to take up pen and paper and write for five or ten minutes she would start writing and humming something shapeless and not quite recognizable as music. Would it have been better if you could recognize a tune, like "Raindrops Keep Falling on My Head"? Probably not. In fact that might have made things worse. As soon as I was able to make eye contact I would place an index finger over my lips. Please, hold that musical thought.

In *Thought and Language* Lev Vygotsky describes "inner speech" as the language small children internalize from conversation and the ongoing babble they hear around them. This language, Vygotsky argues, becomes the basis for verbal thought. He points to "egocentric speech" as evidence of this phenomenon—small children talking aloud to themselves as they play, for example, trying out the words, thinking out loud. Similarly, humming is a kind of egocentric music; the individual's "inner music" is externalized, performed for no one in particular, a performance that often accompanies another activity.

Eventually egocentric speech gives way to "transactional" uses of language—conversation, questions, orders, complaints. We learn not to talk to ourselves when we are around others. To do so is funny. I mean, you know, *funny*. Egocentric music, on the other hand, seems to hang in there. There is a wacky scene in Arthur Miller's *Death of a Salesman* in which Biff and Happy argue about whistling in elevators, with the implication that it is a childish and mildly antisocial behavior. In medical literature on obsessive-compulsive disorder there are plenty of cases of hummers humming, instances that go beyond merely trying out the notes of a song: nonmusical humming, exhalations, and whistling—in short, music and sound meant for no one, music and sound no one wants to hear.

WHY DO WE MAKE MUSIC? What on earth is it for?

Darwin provides us with an evolutionary explanation. In *The Descent of Man* he writes: "When we treat of sexual selection we shall see that primeval man, or rather some early progenitor of man, probably first used his voice in producing true musical cadences, that is in singing. . . . This power would have been especially exerted during the courtship of the sexes,—would have expressed various emotions, such as love, jealousy, triumph,—and would have served as a challenge to rivals." Primeval man on the make, making music. Other theories about why we make music have to do with social cohesion. Music unites us. Hymns create moments of shared spiritual communion. (I know people who weep when they hear their country's national anthem.) Rock songs at concerts and parties and wedding receptions bring us to our feet and stir us to sing along, strum air guitar, and say *Woot! Woot!*

Girls were a secondary motive in my wanting to learn guitar. First and foremost I wanted to play the iconic riff in the Beatles' "Day Tripper."

I was in the seventh grade when I bought an acoustic guitar for twelve dollars from a kid in my class named Eddie Maurer. He brought it to school one Friday in a paper bag. The next week I started lessons with Phil Woodcock. Phil lived down the road. Thursdays after school, with my new guitar clamped under my arm, I walked down to his house, where his mother, whom I remember as a dead ringer for Eleanor Roosevelt, let me in and pointed me to the basement. Phil's studio was an overheated, carpeted room down there. On the other side of one wall, at regular intervals, the furnace clicked on and roared.

I learned to tune the guitar. I learned about the body and neck, the bridge and frets. Phil handed me a book by Mel Bay, with pictures of chords I would need to learn. To explain what a chord progression was he played G, C, D on his guitar. It sounded just like "Hang On, Sloopy" and a dozen other songs I heard on the radio. I took heart. Back home I didn't really play the guitar. I suffered it, squashing the strings against the neck of the guitar with tender fingers. No one, least of all Phil, prepared me for the pain involved in learning to play.

At my fourth lesson he must have sensed I was discouraged. He asked how it was going.

Good, I lied. "The strings hurt," I said.

"You'll get calluses." He showed me the fingertips on his left hand. He said it would take a while.

How long? Could I wait that long?

I played a few chords for him, feeling beads of perspiration form under my shirt and roll down my sides.

"Here's a new progression," he said. "And a new tune." It was D, G, A. He started playing a song popular at the time. Maybe not popular. It was on the radio. He strummed and hummed, and I felt a knot tightening inside me somewhere.

"Is that—?"

"Yes," he said. "You've heard this one."

I had. It was the Singing Nun. Phil strummed the chords and sang these words: *"Dominique, nique, nique ,/ over the land he plods / And sings a little song . . ."* Good God, not that.

Half-hour lessons cost a dollar fifty. It was three dollars for the Mel Bay book. Counting lessons, book, and the guitar, I had invested over twenty dollars and a month of my time. I wasn't much closer to "Day Tripper" than I was the day I brought the guitar home. I decided to go it alone.

It took months of practice, but I eventually got good enough to play those iconic notes of "Day Tripper." The riff didn't sound like much on my twelve-dollar guitar. When I played it a few times for friends at school I noticed that in a matter of seconds they lost interest. I wasn't creating much social cohesion. It wasn't exactly a campfire song. But I kept going.

WE PLAY MUSIC AND sing songs to make love happen and to enjoy social communion, certainly, but we also do it for ourselves. You bake bread to eat, but there's joy in the making. I wonder if music is part of the human creature. Writing about birdsong in *Lives of the Cell*, Lewis Thomas says, "Behind the glossaries of warning calls, alarms, mating messages, pronouncements of territory, calls for recruitment, and demands for dispersal, there is redundant, elegant sound that is unaccountable as part of the working day. The thrush in my backyard sings down his nose in meditative, liquid runs of melody, over and over again, and I have the strongest impression that he does this for his own pleasure." And so it may be for humans. We sing, we strum, we whistle and hum for lots of reasons, perhaps chief among them because it feels good.

For some time now I've been trying to identify a piece of music stuck in my head. These days we would call it an earworm. It's in someone's classical catalog, guitar and two flutes, I'm guessing Bach or one of his contemporaries. There's an app for this: Mobile LaLa search, Midomi, Shazam, SoundHound, Tunatic. Supposedly all I need to do is hum a few bars. If the tune is out there, and if it's digital, the app will identify it. Sometime soon, somewhere private, in my home or in my car, I'll hum the tune or whistle it into my phone, cross my fingers, and hope.

# 2

# Shorty

MY WIFE AND I are having breakfast one morning at a local restaurant. In this establishment you stand in line and place your order at the cash register. You take a number, find a table, and wait for your food. We're here early this day. The restaurant is full of men. It's the power-breakfast hour.

While we wait for our food we watch more men come in, many of them dressed in summer-business casual. A couple tables over, two guys with a laptop talk in hushed tones. At the table next to us a guy leans over a legal pad checking his notes. He's wearing a black and white gingham shirt, jeans, and running shoes. He's got serious, shiny, freshly-combed-back Gordon Gecko hair. In a couple minutes he's joined by another guy in jeans. Their meeting begins.

I'm spreading jam on toast when a new arrival catches my attention. He's on the short side, maybe five feet five inches, wearing gray dress slacks and a blue long-sleeved Oxford shirt open at the neck. And shiny oxblood loafers. No socks. I might not notice this last detail if it weren't for the fact that his pants are a half, maybe a full inch, too short.

I look at my wife, nod in his direction. "That's unfortunate."

"What?"

"That guy there," I say, "with his bare ankles exposed."

She tells me to lower my voice.

"Look at his pants," I whisper. "I don't know how he expects to get ahead in the world with pants like that."

She turns back to her egg sandwich. "He looks like he's doing all right."

"He looks funny."

"You're obsessed."

"A short man in short pants," I say, "is shooting himself in the foot. I can't bear to look."

"Obsessed."

It's partly her mother's fault.

My mother-in-law was trained in Italy as a tailor. For years she altered my pants for me. I'd bring them to the house, change into them in what used to be my wife's bedroom, and stand on a stool in the family room while my mother-in-law, with three or four pins pinched in the corner of her mouth, talked to me in Italian as she pulled the inseam, measured and marked the hem. The same way she fixed pants for my father-in-law, who was about my height, and for her brother, who was also about my height. Perfect. The right amount of break. Just the right length. My pants never looked so good.

"Just watch," I say, "when he sits down."

"Eat your breakfast."

I take a bite of toast, tell her a short man ought to know better.

ALONG WITH SEXISM AND racism, heightism is a fact of life today. Heightism cuts across race and gender. It's not a just a man's world. It's a tall man's world.

Researchers at Harvard University, in Project Implicit, look at heightism as a naturally occurring implicit bias, shaped by "thoughts and feelings outside conscious awareness and control." And, really, this bias is evident from birth forward. We marvel at big newborns. "He has such long legs!" We congratulate children for being tall. Tall boys rule on the playground, are at an advantage in sports, and are regarded by girls as more attractive, more *desirable* than not-tall boys. A tall boy can swing both ways, dating tall and short girls, unlike a not-tall boy, way down there on the left end of the bell curve, confronting the grim reality of standard deviations. In his adult years a tall man will earn, on average, up to $5,500 a year more than a not-tall man. Tall men will rise to positions of power, become presidents and CEOs. In the 1988 presidential debate, behind his lectern next to George H. W. Bush, Michael Dukakis, five feet eight inches tall, stood on a box to appear presidential.

"We see a tall person," Malcolm Gladwell writes, "and we swoon."

Granted, some history has been made and written by not-tall men. Aristotle was five feet five. Alexander the Great was a modest five feet six. Voltaire and Beethoven rose to five feet three, while James Madison and Mahatma Gandhi, towering political geniuses, measured just five feet four. Joseph Stalin, who was five feet five, murdered millions. Frodo Baggins is a mere three feet six. Of course Tom Cruise comes to mind as well, a measly five feet seven, exploiting all the magic of filmmaking to appear taller than he is. Lately he is Jack Reacher tall on screen, whereas the Lee Child character is six feet six in the novels. Like that of Michael Dukakis, Cruise's shortness, in the view of filmmakers, and no doubt in his own view, needs to be fixed.

TO BE NOT TALL, and I mean radically not tall, two standard deviations (six inches) or more below the mean (five feet ten inches), is regarded as an illness. It has a name: idiopathic short stature (ISS). These days that illness has a cure—recombinant human growth hormone, affectionately known as rhGH. Dr. Juan F. Sotos, a pediatric endocrinologist at the Nationwide Children's Hospital, observes in a study published in 2010: "Growth hormone treatment significantly improved the adult height of children with ISS, sometimes with an improvement of up to 4 inches." Four inches? At the age of fifteen, what I would have given for a pitcher of rhGH, a life-improving elixir.

There is no ITS (idiopathic tall stature). If you are two standard deviations above the mean you are probably just considered a born leader. The tallest man in history, as far as we know, was

Robert Pershing Wallow, born in Illinois on February 22, 1918. He grew to be eight feet eleven inches tall. In Rotterdam a statue was erected in honor of Rigardus Rijnhout, who was seven feet six. The Dutch, statistically the tallest people on earth today, decided to commemorate the life of Rijnhout, "the Giant of Rotterdam," whose life, it must be noted, was not without difficulty and who died at thirty-six.

AT CARNIVALS AND AMUSEMENT PARKS, next to some rides there is a height scale. You must be at least this tall—twenty-four inches, thirty-six inches, forty-eight inches—to ride this ride. That scale, or one like it, is encoded in our genes, deeply submerged in our consciousness. If you are this height—one or two standard deviations below the mean—you should probably be accompanied by a tall person.

Some years ago I bought a bad bottle of wine at a local shop. Around this time I had undertaken a project. Get to know wine. Learn to like it. My approach was to concentrate on California wine, reds only. It had sort of worked. After a couple years of practice I could select Cabernets for ten dollars that I liked. Some days I decided to live large and spent twelve dollars. I whiffed corks. I swirled and tasted and said things like, "This wine has great legs." "This wine is full bodied." I began to feel confident. Foreign wines remained intimidating. I couldn't pronounce the names on the labels, didn't know the grapes or the geography of those countries.

One day, feeling adventurous, I decided to try a wine from Spain. Home from the wine store, I set the bottle on the counter.

My wife looked at me. "What's that?"

"It's something or other," I said. I didn't try to say the name. I yanked the cork, squeezed it between my thumb and forefinger, suggested we let the wine breathe.

Outside the grill was hot. I tossed meat on it, to follow a dish of pasta and accompany a few vegetables. When the meat was done we sat down to eat.

At the first sip of wine I had questions.

"Do you think this tastes good?"

"What's it supposed to taste like?

"Spain, I guess."

"I agree. It tastes strange."

"Would you say 'corky'?"

"What does cork taste like?"

"Do you think it tastes old? past its prime? like maybe it wasn't cellared properly?"

My wife looked at the bottle. "Do they cellar a wine that costs twelve bucks?"

While we were talking our neighbor came through our yard walking his dog. I invited him to taste the wine. He swirled it in a clean glass, held it up to the light. He asked me, Didn't I find the color brownish? He smelled the wine, took a taste, executed a shallow gargle, and swallowed. "Bad," he said. He poured another taste, repeated the process. "Bad," he said again. "I'd take it back."

I'd never taken a wine back before, but it seemed like it would be a pretty common occurrence. On television and in the movies people sent wine back all the time. I figured, What the hell.

Next day I handed the guy at the wine shop the bottle, half full, plugged shut with its questionable cork.

"I think I got a bad bottle," I said.

He was tall, portly, bearded. I think his specialty in the store was cigars. I shopped there once in a while. I wouldn't say I was a regular customer, a known customer. There was another guy, smaller, slimmer, more alcoholic looking, whom I usually talked to. He wasn't there that day. The bearded guy lowered his glasses to the bridge of his nose, squinted, and read the label. Then he pulled out the cork and examined it.

"If the wine was bad," he said, "why did you drink half of it?"

Oh no. I felt the tops of my ears warm with embarrassment. I told him the story, my wife and I trying it, then the neighbor, who thought it looked brownish.

Tall bearded guy lifted the bottle. The glass was dark brown. You could barely make out the contents. He sniffed at the top of the bottle. Then he smelled it again.

"There's nothing wrong with this wine," he said.

"It tastes bad," I said. "It's the taste."

He smelled it a third time, shook his head. "There's nothing wrong with this wine."

We talked for a minute. No, I didn't have a receipt. Yes, it was most certainly their wine, I said. I'd checked the shelf. I told him it seemed like bad business: it was an inexpensive wine to lose a customer over. Maybe because it was an inexpensive wine he didn't mind losing a customer.

"Well," I said finally, "all right." Leaving the wine on the counter I walked out of the store, seething. The customer is always right.

The not-tall customer is also always right.

I couldn't help but wonder: what if I had been six feet tall?

Maybe this wasn't heightism at work. Maybe that internalized height scale (*you must be at least this tall . . .*) had nothing to do with what happened. Maybe bearded guy was just having a bad day. Maybe he was a really nice guy; he was just a nice guy, as Garrison Keillor said once, to other people.

I never went back to that store.

Somehow that didn't seem like enough.

IN 2010 THE NATIONAL Bureau of Economic Research published a study entitled "Short Criminals: Short Stature and Crime in Early America." Examining data from the Pennsylvania prison population between 1826 and 1876, the study concludes: "Consistent with a theory in which height can be a source of labor market disadvantage, criminals in early America were shorter than the average American, and individual crime hazards decreased in height." Oh, really? This correlation was seen by researchers in Sweden as well. Published in the *International Journal of Epidemiology*, their study examined a pool of 760,000 men between 1980 and 1992, men who, in lieu of jail sentences, were required to serve in the military. The study concludes: "The shortest of men were twice as likely to be convicted of a violent crime as the tallest." Many of these men, the researchers suggest, were also stupid.

THERE ARE, IT SHOULD be noted, benefits to being small. I fit in a bed. I have a low center of gravity, which means that as I age I will be less in danger of falling than a not-short person. Short people look younger and tend to live longer than not-short people. On a hot day I can stand next to a not-short person and use him for shade.

When I was six years old, a mere speck of a human being, I got to visit the set of the Professor Von Clobber show. My brother, two years older, was in Cub Scouts. His pack carpooled with a couple moms to the WNEM studio, where the afternoon kids' show was broadcast live. I remember being mildly terrified. The set was small and brightly lit. It smelled of dust and electric power chords. The Professor was a tall, unpleasant man who seemed bored and grouchy, a man, any kid could sense, who did not like children. I was a tagalong that day, the smallest kid in the group. One of the mothers seated me in the front row so I could see.

Not long ago I took a long ride on an airplane. Next to me in coach, in the window seat, was a very genial fellow from Atlanta. He was tall and thin, I'm guessing six feet four inches or more. I told him about my work, he told me about his. We commiserated about the inconveniences of air travel. Throughout the flight he squirmed and folded and unfolded his long limbs. He asked to get up three times. By the third time I felt like he had begun to make a pest of himself. Eventually I was able to put him out of my mind, shifting my seat back and stretching out. That day, at thirty-six thousand feet, I was my own private rewards program. It was good to be short.

# 3

# Bridge

IN THE END IT all came down to two points.

My freshman year of high school the wrestling team had no one to put in the ninety-five-pound weight class. That meant at every meet the team would forfeit that match, giving the opposition five points for free and an automatic advantage in the final score.

The coach at the time was a guy named Jack Curl. He had short blond hair and an easy smile. In the fall he coached football. That's where his heart was. He also taught gym, although "taught" somehow seems like the wrong word. "Moderated" or "presided over" or "benignly neglected" might be more accurate. I recall him walking around the gym holding a clipboard, blowing on a referee whistle he wore around his neck, yelling at kids. Winter semesters he coached wrestling, which as the phys ed teacher he probably had to do. I don't think he knew much about the sport. He referred to it as "wrastling."

Activities in gym class corresponded roughly to the teams the school fielded in formal competition. In the fall we played football, always flag or touch football to minimize bloodshed. After football season came crab soccer (actual soccer had not been discovered yet in the Midwest) and badminton and tumbling (a primitive form of gymnastics). In the winter there was a lot of basketball, of course, which Coach Curl did not coach or seem to care much about. Then came the unit on wrestling.

"I want you on the wrestling team," he told me one day in gym class. I was spidering up the peg board. A lightweight, I was also good at rope-climb. "I need a ninety-five-pounder," he said.

It was the winter of 1967. I was learning to play the guitar. The group I had formed with three other guys had already played a few sock hops. We were capable of ragged renditions of a few three-chord wonders—"Hang On, Sloopy," "Louie Louie," and "Gloria." My favorite song at the time was "Psychotic Reaction," by Count Five. We couldn't play it. It was an aspirational song. The point is, in those days I saw myself on stage in the cafetorium, not on a mat in the gymnasium wearing a leotard and tights, with my face pressed into some guy's armpit or crotch.

"Bailey," the coach said another day, "You're going to be my ninety-five-pounder."

"I don't weigh ninety-five pounds," I said. I was more like eighty-four pounds. I'm pretty sure I had not yet achieved five feet in height either.

I'd been to meets. My brother, two years ahead of me, was on the team. I'd heard the splat of flesh when boys hit the mat, heard the grunts and groans, seen the straining muscles and grotesque red faces. I'd heard the stories about kids having to "make weight." That usually meant starving themselves to get down to 112 or 120 or 132, to 145 or 154. One guy on the team, in addition to starving himself, relied on laxatives, which he took for a few days before meet day, when he showed up on weight, dehydrated and diminished but ready to go.

A few weeks before the first wrestling meet Coach Curl announced that I would be wrestling every member of class until I agreed to be on the team. We were upstairs on the mezzanine in the gym, where we'd been tumbling for a few weeks and where the class would wrestle. He smiled when he said this. It was a disarming smile. I played along. What choice did I have? That day in second-hour gym class I wrestled kids bigger than I was, some of them twice my size, who took it as a joke and pinned me without malice and with minimal violence. This went on for a week. At first I found it funny. I admit I kind of liked being wanted. There was a U.S. Army poster at the time, and ads on TV as the war in Vietnam began to expand, Uncle Sam pointing and saying "I WANT YOU." It felt sort of like that.

A week before the first meet I gave in.

I went to three days of practice. I knew a few of the basics about an individual match, three two-minute periods, and I knew a few takedowns, a few holds. I also knew that running away was not a strategy. I would have to lock arms and attempt to subdue my opponent. Or at the very least fend him off manfully.

My first match was on a Thursday night. It was an away meet, in Shepherd.

Matches were organized in ascending order. Every night the ninety-five-pound weight class went first. That first night it all happened pretty fast.

The kid I was going to wrestle looked across the mat at me and sized me up. He was no freshman. He had the hulking body mass of a full ninety-five-pounder. He also had the vengeful look of a kid who had been beaten up more than a few times. We walked to the center of the mat and shook hands. When the ref blew the whistle my opponent lowered his body into a crouch. He held out his hands toward me. His right hand shook in midair. It was like the twitching of a snake's tongue. I tried to adopt a similar pose, lowering my body, establishing what Coach Curl called my "power center." The kid and I moved once counterclockwise around the center of the mat, maintaining distance. We'd just reversed direction when he lunged for my knees and wrapped me up. I went down.

He smelled like soup. He moved fast. The next sixty seconds was an abbreviated summary in scoring for high school wrestling: takedown (2 points for my opponent), near fall (3 points for my opponent), escape (1 point for me). Another takedown and I was on the mat on my stomach. On top of me the kid felt like an octopus, all tangling appendages working. He executed a chicken-wing maneuver, aptly named, and I was on my back at the edge of the mat, inches from out of bounds. He skidded me away from the line and bore down on me even harder. I strained to keep one of my shoulders off the mat. I could hear my teammates yelling Bridge! Bridge! Bridge! The ref lowered himself to our level, his head right next to ours, watching, checking, waiting. Then his hand smacked the mat.

I was pinned.

My opponent and I stood up. He was smiling, kind of dancing beside me. My legs were shaking. I looked over at Coach Curl, who shook his head once.

Pinned. In the first period.

It was kind of like being knocked out. It was five points for Shepherd, same as if our team had forfeited the match.

I slunk off the mat and flung myself onto a folding chair, crossed my arms over my chest. The meet proceeded. We lost by more than five points.

With no help from me.

The next two or three matches were much the same. First period pins. Five points I contributed to the opposing team. Same as a forfeit.

"THEY WEIGH MORE THAN YOU," my brother said. We were riding home after a meet one night. I had algebra homework to do. It was snowing. Maybe they would have to close school next day, I thought, on account of snow. I hoped so. I wouldn't have to go to school.

"They weigh more than me," I said.

He did the math. "More than 10 percent more. That's a lot."

Some of them, I pointed out, were also older.

"Some of them," he said.

At practices after school Coach Curl said I needed to train harder.

The 120 showed me how to bridge, lying on his back, using his legs and head to lift his body off the mat. "That's how you keep your shoulders off the mat," he said. "That's how you don't get pinned." The way I saw it, I'd have to hold that bridge for most of two, four, possibly six minutes. It looked like a long invitation to having your neck broken.

The 145 showed me his favorite hold, the figure four. "I like to lock it in," he said, "right around the guy's waist, then lean into it, and ride him to the mat."

When I said it looked like it hurt, he said it did, that was the point.

The 165 asked me how come I didn't have any hair on my legs.

The 180 said, "Can't you gain some weight? You gotta eat more."

There were other guys on the team that lost matches, a few who got pinned. There were a few who had gone undefeated. I was the only one on the team who had lost every match.

The 103, who had wrestled at 95 the previous year, said what everyone else on the team thought: Just don't get pinned. If I went all three periods and simply lost, the opposing team got three points, not five. If I didn't get pinned, in wrestling math I was only two negative points.

"One thing about wrestlers is if they get on their back, it's not over—it just got interesting." So says Zane Kesey, whose father, Ken Kesey, was a wrestling phenomenon in high school and college. "You get fierce," Zane Kesey adds. In a 2012 article in *The Telegraph* novelist John Irving, another writer-wrestler all his life, explains his passion: "I had a particular affinity for wrestling and it [had] a lot to do with being small and being combative—and being angry." Irving recalls his high school coach telling him, "An underdog is in a position to take a healthy bite."

I was an underdog, all right. But if there was one thing I wasn't, it was combative. I was underweight, undercombative, underangry.

"I NEED TO GAIN some weight," I said at the dinner table one night. It was the end of a quiet meal. We'd had a home meet by then. My father had come to watch. He'd seen me get pinned early and fast.

My brother had won his match. He passed me a platter.

I dragged a pile of mashed potatoes onto my plate, squashed them into a pancake with my fork, and spread some butter on them. I asked my mother what was for dessert.

"Are you hungry?" my dad asked.

"I need to gain some weight," I said.

"Are you hungry?" he asked again.

"Coach says a couple pounds could make a difference."

"Cake," my mother said. "Chocolate."

"What I don't like about this wrestling," my father said, "is the weight loss and weight gain."

At least, my brother pointed out, I didn't have to take Ex-Lax.

"It's unnatural," my father said. "It's not healthy."

"He's getting better," my brother said, pushing a slice of bread in my direction.

I said I was trying. But, really, I wasn't getting better. I was getting pinned. And I wasn't really trying. I trained, I ate, I gained a pound. I practiced bridging. I tried to grow hair on my legs. Two more matches, two more pins. The latter was a second-period pin. It was progress. It was my personal best. No one was much inclined to celebrate. That included me.

I WAS IN GRIDLEY Music one Saturday around this time. Monte, the guy behind the counter, had sold me an electric guitar. He wore turtlenecks. He had sideburns. He reminded me of Peter, Paul, and Mary, one of those guys. In another year Monte would be coming to the store wearing beads around his neck. When he asked how the band was doing I told him that I was taking some time off from music, that I was on the wrestling team.

He burst out laughing. "You?" he said. "What the hell you doing that for?"

I told him I was still playing the guitar, just on my own, which was the truth.

He said he wanted to see my muscles.

"Some other time," I said.

"Come on, take off your coat. Let's see your muscles."

I said I was just giving wrestling a try. It was an experiment.

"You killing them?"

"I'm doing all right."

"That's what's important," he said. "Hey, I got something cool to show you." He reached for a box on a shelf behind the counter, opened it, and set a small black device on the counter. It was the size of a transistor radio. On the side of it were a dial and a small white toggle switch.

"You plug it into your guitar," he said, "flip this switch and you got fuzz, man."

He led me into the back room. "Show him this," he said to a tech working back there.

The tech plugged the device into a guitar, connected it to an amplifier, and played a buzzy, highly distorted chord. It didn't sound like much.

"Listen to this," the tech said.

He cranked the volume on the amp.

"You got your Rolling Stones' 'Satisfaction.'" He played the opening notes. "You got your Beatles' 'Think for Yourself.'" He played the opening notes. "And you got your Count Five." He played the opening notes of "Psychotic Reaction."

And it only cost twenty bucks.


MIDSEASON I WENT THE full three periods and didn't get pinned. It was a meet at home. You could say I benefited from home-mat advantage. Maybe that's true. When the ref raised my opponent's hand there was no applause, except from my father and a few guys on the team. The number ticked on the scoreboard: Buena Vista 3, Freeland 0.

The next week something wonderful happened. We took the bus on a Thursday night to Bullock Creek. At weigh-in I saw the opposing team had no one to wrestle in the ninety-five-pound weight class. Five points for our team. Also a full reprieve from the weekly humiliation.

"Way to go, man," a couple teammates said to me. "You won."

A few weeks later there was another forfeit. Five more points for our team. Just being there, just showing up and pulling on my tights, I'd helped.

I went 2-14 that season. There was no point in doing the math. I knew I was a net loss for the Falcons. But in Coach Curl's twisted and cruel calculus the sum of my losses was a gain for the team. And I'd gone the distance in a varsity sport. My freshman year I got a varsity letter, an F.

That spring I heard Jimi Hendrix for the first time. His album "Are You Experienced" was released on May 12, 1967. The radio was playing Buffalo Springfield's "For What It's Worth" and Jefferson Airplane's "White Rabbit." The Louie-Louie band I'd played in fell apart. I formed a new band with a couple guys and used my new fuzz tone to play "Purple Haze." My voice was changing, but I still had a falsetto good enough for our cover of James Brown's "I Feel Good."

That summer the guy who wrestled 132 on the team graduated and went to Vietnam. A few guys from our town were already coming back from there, some of them pretty damaged, returning to a country going crazy.

The next year, when I might have won, when I might have mopped up at ninety-five, I did not wrestle. It was 1968.

# 4

# Call It a Dance

I'VE BEEN THINKING LATELY about the degradation of dance. Not how we are degraded by it, although some of us certainly look foolish. I mean how we have degraded it. When was dance reduced to rhythmic flopping?

What occasioned these reflections on dance is *Caro, Diario,* the 1993 Nanni Moretti film I watched again recently. In the opening minutes, in a section called "Vespa," Moretti tours Rome on his *motorino,* talking about what he loves: the emptiness of Rome during the summer, the houses and neighborhoods. He provides wry commentary along the way, on social class and politics and contemporary life. He feels separate from the majority of people, he says. He feels disconnected.

Then, rounding a curve, with the sound of music rising in the soundtrack, he adds, "In realtà il mio sogno è sempre stato quello di saper ballare bene. *Flashdance* si chiamava quel film che mi ha cambiato definitivamente la vita." *In reality my dream has always been to be a good dancer.* Flashdance *changed my life.*

In the next moment he comes to a stop on his Vespa at the edge of an outdoor dance party. A live band is performing. Dozens of couples are dancing the merengue.

The music and movement are infectious, irresistibly so. You can't look on and not want to do that. And yet Moretti, like those watching the film, is little more than a spectator. He says, "E invece alla fine mi riduco sempre a guardare, che è anche bello, però è tutt'un'altra cosa." *In the end all I can do is watch, which is great, but not at all the same thing.*

IN THE MIDSIXTIES I learned one basic dance step. This was junior high school. A couple days a week we had lunch hour a-go-go. Kids brought their forty-fives to school. Danny Leman or Ronnie Fritz checked out a record player from the AV room. There were ten or fifteen minutes before classes resumed. In a back corner of the cafetorium girls danced, some of them in white go-go boots. They danced the pony, the jerk, the mashed potato, there was a little bit of shimmy, an occasional hitchhike. And all the while the boys sat and watched, mildly terrified, waiting for the slow song.

There were plenty of slow songs: baby slow songs—"Be My Baby," "Ooo Baby Baby"; sad slow songs—"Only Love Can Break a Heart," "A Town Without Pity," "Don't Let the Sun Catch You Crying"; and tragedy slow songs—"The Leader of the Pack," "Tell Laura I Love Her," "Where Oh Where Can My Baby Be." Slow dancing contained all the awkwardness and terror of adolescence, yet in terms of performance it was relatively safe. If nothing else, you could just slowly rock from side to side and call that a dance. Somehow in seventh or eighth grade I learned to do a box step. When Danny or Ronnie or a real DJ decided to slow things down, I could just follow my feet.

High school was much the same: girls doing the fast dances (pony, jerk, potato), boys on the sidelines, still terrified, cautiously waiting for the slow dance.

Leaving aside the obvious gender divide, if you asked someone they would probably say some people can dance, some can't. Most can't. It's sort of like math.

PLATO SAID WE SHOULD get up and bust a move (though not exactly in those words).

For him an uneducated person was "danceless." Graham Pont, a historical musicologist, explores the centrality of dance in classical education. He observes, "Through dance (which included posture, deportment, gesture, facial expression, and other bodily movement) the young Greek learned not only to be quick, strong, agile, dexterous, and graceful but (most importantly) to imitate and internalize the characteristic rhythms, movements, and attitude of the ideally noble Hellene." Dance, furthermore, did in fact have a mathematical component, relating to musical scale and the alignment of the planets, what came to be known as "the harmony of the spheres." If you were young and Greek and wanted to understand the cosmos, math and dance were where it was at.

Our response to music and the deep pleasure we take in rhythmic movement seem to be innate. According to *Psychology Today*, there is a "natural desire known in the scientific literature as 'entrainment.' Entrainment occurs when resonant fields rhythmically synchronize together, such as brain waves, circadian rhythms, lunar and solar cycles, breathing, circulation, and rhythms found in the nervous system. It is a way the body experiences the sensation of feeling understood, seen, and not alone." That happens when you dance.

The problem is developing and sustaining these feelings. A recent study presented in *Scientific American* reveals what happens to children and their desire to dance as they grow older. In a controlled experiment kids aged eleven or twelve were 75 percent more likely to *avoid* singing and dancing than children aged three or four. The researchers attribute this difference to "terror of performance."

"SO," MY SON SAYS to me, "you've still got that chicken thing going."

We're at a niece's wedding reception. The tables have been cleared, the lights lowered. The DJ has cranked the volume on his sound system. My wife and I are coming off the dance floor, where we just danced to two Motowns in a row.

"Chicken?" I say.

He folds his arms into wings, gives them a couple flaps.

"You do do that," my wife says to me, "when you dance."

"Yeah, so?" I look from her to my son, who nods in agreement. Like, *It's something you need to work on.* Like, *No more walking around the house in your underwear. No more mixed drinks in the morning.*

"Mick Jagger," he says.

Right, I think. Mick Jagger does that. "So?"

Another nod, both of them in sync. So I'm not Mick Jagger.

The DJ has cued up "Living the Vida Loca," a song I really like, a great dance number. I pull at my wife. If this guy is like other wedding DJ's he'll play old stuff early in the evening, then transition to the new music I don't know, don't understand, and don't really like. One feels a sense of urgency.

"You also snap your fingers when you dance," my wife says. "A lot." She glances at my son. He gives me his gentle judgmental nod.

"You do do that," he says. "A lot."

I tell my wife to hurry up. My son and his girlfriend join us on the floor. At some point they're doing a dance together that involves him spazzing rhythmically and her giving him chest compressions. Near them a couple is doing a dance that calls to mind lawn sprinklers. And of course there is a lot of rhythmic flopping. My wife, a good dancer, returns to her Soul Train roots. I sort of imitate her, but not very well.

According to a T-shirt I saw recently, we're supposed to dance like there's no one watching. I flap and snap, looking around me, gazing upon various interpretations of the harmony of the spheres. Not danceless. But almost.

# 5

# Tilt

WHEN I WAS IN elementary school, one of the perks of getting your picture taken was you got a free plastic pocket comb. It was green. It had the photography company name printed on the side in white lettering. The favored cuts, offered by all three barbers in town, were the Flattop, the Butch, the Princeton, and the Regular, none of which required a lot of maintenance. Nevertheless, on picture day there was a lot of combing and sprucing and sidelong self-regarding glances at windows.

If I could I escaped to the bathroom on those days with Joe Hrcka. Back then the evolution of "product" for men's hair was still primitive at best. There were Vitalis, Brylcreem, and a few other fragrant unguents with the consistency and viscosity of motor oil. Joe Hrcka was a visionary. He applied a handful of that foamy white school bathroom soap to his bangs (he wore a Regular), combing them straight out from his forehead forklift style. Now that I think of it the Forklift could easily have been added to the menu of cuts. This cross between mousse and gel worked for ten or fifteen minutes, usually losing hold before you got in front of the camera. It's probably just as well.

On picture day I felt hope and dread in equal measures. *This is the year. Finally I'll look good.* Past years my teeth had looked too big, or I had an oversized freckle on my nose, or it seemed like my neck didn't fit, or my Princeton looked, and probably was, hacked. You sat for the photo, and then you made your wager, betting with the size of your order—wallet-size, three-by-fives, five-by-sevens, an eight-by-ten—that your photo would actually become currency you could use to trade for other photos. The photographer took one shot. One roll of the dice. Then you waited.

And one morning, long after you had forgotten about picture day, the blue eleven-by-fourteen-inch envelopes were delivered to your class. In each envelope was a small window in which your likeness appeared. You held your breath and finally looked.

*Yes, that's me.*

*Rats.*

For a week or so after school pictures arrived you swapped photos. Often it was a joyless, perfunctory transaction. You would hand someone your picture, they would look and shake their head with a facial expression that said, *Too bad!* For a week or two you'd see combs on desks, in kids' back pockets, then on the floor in the classroom, the hallway, and the gym. Soon enough they disappeared altogether.

But the pictures remained.

WHEN MY BROTHER AND I cleared out my parents' house this past year, after they had both died, we came upon the drawer. We knew it was there. In that drawer were all those photographs, many of which only a mother could love. Looking at them, I wondered what impact digital photography will have on memory. These days there is a profusion of images (we don't say "picture" so much anymore), not hundreds, but tens of thousands of them, but they are not in a drawer. They are pixels and bytes saved in ephemeral vessels that need much more attention and care than a drawer, media that are subject to arbitrary destruction through virus, fizzle, and crash. And searching those vessels—floppies, zips, thumb drives, hard drives, detachables—is nowhere near as pleasurable as sitting at a kitchen table shuffling through envelopes of black-and-whites and stacks of curled color prints, on the back of which a person—a classmate, a family member, possibly you yourself—wrote in blue or black ink a few words in wobbly cursive.

*Fifth grade.*

CERTAINLY WE ARE MORE image-conscious than ever before.

I recently updated my profile picture on Facebook after reading an article about head tilt on *Slate*. In the photo I replaced I was in full tilt.

I get tilt from my mother. Browse through family photos, especially those with epochal significance inviting a pose—family reunions, birthday parties, holiday gatherings, weddings—and there she is, her head tilted back, her mouth slightly open. I do it too. I think of it as our airway management pose.

*Chin down*, I tell myself now when the camera comes out. *And shut your mouth.*

I remember trying to train my face when I was a kid, looking in the mirror, smiling on purpose, calibrating lip lift, mouth width, just the right reveal of tooth. It was useless. I couldn't reproduce a look. My face and I were not on the same page. But that was youth. Adults, I think, have sufficient self-control, they know their faces well enough to execute on demand the same natural-seeming, camera-ready smile virtually every time.

But what's with the lean?

The head tilt in question, the one that motivated my profile photo swap, is not the airway management tilt. It's a lateral lean.

In my profile photo on the outs I'm leaning left in a way that could be scientifically interesting. A lateral lean *means* something. In a recent study media expert Lev Manovich and strategic interaction designer Daniel Goddemeyer examined photos from New York, Bangkok, Moscow, São Paulo, and Berlin, 640 selfies from each city, subjecting them to rigorous scientific analysis. They found 50 percent more lateral tilt in women (12.3 degrees) than in men (8.2 degrees). According to a monumental study at the University of São Paulo, lateral lean is seen as an "appeasement gesture." That's not all. In both men and women "greater levels of beauty but lower levels of happiness were attributed to [persons] with the head tilted than to [those] with the head upright."

At Cambridge University researchers have messed with the Mona Lisa, using digital technology to give her head tilt. They conclude that with a certain degree of cant, her vexing smile becomes even more mysterious. They note in the *Journal of Nonverbal Behavior*: "Laterally tilted to the left of the vertical (i.e., the same direction as her glance) produced more pronounced effects of her smile."

Head tilt makes us look more beautiful, more vexy, less happy.

In my leaning photo, which exceeds 12.3 degrees, possibly clocking as high at 15 or 16 degrees, I won't speak to the beauty quotient, but I happen to know my happiness factor is way up there, almost off the charts. Behind me in the original photo lies the Tyrrhenian Sea, a shiny blue jewel, and in the distance the Sicilian town of Castellammare del Golfo. Beside me in the original photo is my wife. I'm leaning hard, in an affectionate husbandly manner, in her direction. (I would show you the whole picture, but unfortunately her eyes are closed.)

When we got home I cropped the photo and uploaded it to Facebook. Sometime after that I read the Slate article and noticed the lean. That's when doubt crept in. I cropped the photo again and, using a photo editor, straightened my head for a less appeasing look.

It's a little embarrassing, all this cropping, all this attention to the pose, all this vain self-celebration. Freud thought of narcissism as "the delusion of being watched." Follow me on Facebook. Follow me on Twitter. Let's update the definition: narcissism is the delusion of being followed.

But wait a minute.

Rembrandt painted sixty self-portraits. Just think how long that took, how much of his lifetime was spent looking at himself on canvas after canvas. That guy was so self-absorbed.

The first photographic selfie? Robert Cornelius, in 1839, held still for anywhere from three to fifteen minutes while his image was captured in a daguerreotype. That's a long time. That's a guy who wanted have his picture taken. Or maybe not. Judging from the image he sat there thinking, *Chin down. And shut your mouth. I'm only going to do this once.*

Selfie technology has come a long way since then. The camera is now ubiquitous. It is our digital mirror. Fix your face, adjust your look, you only have to hold it for a second. Click, view, share. No, wait. Try again. And again. And again. And again.

Click, view. *Straighten.*

Share.

# 6

# Bring Your Horn

EVERY SO OFTEN I find myself doing this thing I call a "Doug Anderson."

A guy I knew in high school, Doug Anderson, drove a 1968 Pontiac Firebird. It was shiny. It was clean. It was red. Any given Saturday afternoon you would see him cruising down Washington Street at a little under the speed limit, both hands on the steering wheel, one at two o'clock and the other at ten o'clock. If ever man and machine were one it was Doug Anderson and his Firebird. Except for one thing. He drove with a certain tilt of his head, canted to the left. It was just a thing he did, I know, but that head tilt made it seem like he was listening for something, a squeak, a sigh of air, a tapping under the hood, a rattle beneath the car. Something wasn't quite right.

A few days after getting my hair cut a suspicion dawns on me. I may have gotten another crooked cut. The hair over my right ear looks longer and thicker than the hair over my left ear. I don't look level. I scrutinize my head in the bathroom mirror and do a Doug Anderson. Am I asymmetrical?

MY THIRD YEAR OF college I sat next to a girl with amazing eyes, one brown, one green. It was a course in existentialism. Most of the semester the professor talked to the wall, lecturing in the direction of a space at the rear of the room, where the ceiling came to a point in one corner. He talked about knights of faith and infinite resignation, about nausea and despair, about being and nothingness.

While he talked I took notes. But mostly I waited for a chance to meet this girl's eyes. By midterm the real point of the course, what I was learning to call its raison d'etre, had become Janelle.

"I'm a business major," she said with a smile the first day of class. She wore linen and smelled like lemons.

"And you're interested in philosophy," I said. Noticing her eyes— and how could you not?—I must have made a face she was used to seeing.

I glanced away, embarrassed, and told her I was I undeclared. When I looked back she was drumming the fingers of her left hand near mine on the table. She wore a wedding ring.

"I don't match," she said.

I looked at her ring finger.

"Yes," she said, "I am."

That settled it. We got to be Tuesday-Thursday afternoon friends. We had this Platonic thing that started, lasted fifteen weeks, and then stopped.

And she let me look. I was one of the lucky people in the world. Two days a week I looked into Janelle's brown and green eyes, and she met my gaze full on.

We're supposed to match. If we have two of something they are supposed to become part of our symmetry—eyes, ears, hands, feet, nostrils. We would like equal parts, but it's rarely the case. There are dominant sides of our brains. Switch hitters are rare. Who writes with either hand? When I shop for shoes I try on both shoes; my left foot is just a tiny bit bigger than the right. And teeth. Only through the art and low-level violence of orthodontics have mouths achieved a semblance of symmetry. When my hair was long, around the time I knew Janelle, I wore it parted in the middle, but usually the part was only middle-ish on my imperfect, slightly asymmetrical head.

IT MAY HAVE BEEN an unconscious desire for symmetry that drew me to music. Five lines on the staff; whole, half and quarter, eighth and sixteenth notes arranged in stately measures. Seven finger holes on top of the recorder, three valves on the trumpet; six strings on the guitar, E string on top, E string on the bottom. I hadn't yet heard of the music of the spheres; the racket made by twenty-six fifth graders wheezing "Ode to Joy" on their recorders barely qualified as music, but there was something in it—tempo, rhythm, melody—that must have held out a promise, to act as a stay against adolescent chaos.

In the high school band I sat next to Jennifer Purvis. She wore glasses, her long brown hair perfectly parted in the middle. She had a wacky sense of humor, and I sensed she liked me as much as I liked her. But I could never work up the courage to ask her out. She was a full three inches taller than I was. We didn't match. On the other side of Purvis was Bob Strecker, a year older, first chair trumpet player who had migrated to the baritone.

The spring I was in the eleventh grade Strecker called me. Did I want to go with him to an audition? Amphagas wanted him to come to a rehearsal. They were looking for horns. "Come with me," he said. "Bring your horn."

Amphagas was the old Count and the Colony.

Count and the Colony had won the 1966 Michigan State Battle of the Bands. They wore Paul-Revere-and-the-Raiders-esque costumes, complete with lace ascots. They had a record. They were on the radio, possibly television. And they had a Hammond organ.

Most bands at that time, if they had a keyboard, it was a Farfisa, a puny-sounding thing a few steps up from a mouth organ, the organ you hear on "96 Tears." Count and the Colony, about to become Amphagas, had Dick Brown. He played a Hammond B-3 through a Leslie. I'd seen them play one set at the Blue Light in Midland (before a bouncer bounced me for being underage). Butch Burden (aka the Count) wailed on "Mustang Sally." But what stood out was that organ, so loud it was like a 707 landing on stage.

This was 1969, the year of Blood, Sweat & Tears. Strecker and I, with his girl Jackie mashed between us in the front seat, had driven down to Adrian College and back, on a school night, to hear David Clayton Thomas sing "God Bless the Child" and "And When I Die" and, most importantly, to hear Lew Soloff's trumpet solo on "Spinning Wheel." That kind of play was within reach for Strecker.

Not me. Driving to the Amphagas audition that afternoon I felt like an impostor.

The band was set up in the back room of a house on the west side of Saginaw. Drums, amplifiers, mic stands, a mess of cords all over the floor. A dusty electric smell hung in the air. Dick Brown leaned over the B-3 keyboard smoking a cigarette and watched us unpack our stuff.

We talked over the watty hum of the PA system. When Strecker got out his trumpet Butch motioned to my horn case, "What is that thing?"

I hauled out my instrument, on loan from Freeland Public Schools.

"It's a French horn," I said.

In tenth grade I had moved from trumpet to French horn. Jennifer Purvis played the French horn.

"French?" Butch started to laugh. "Man, that thing's strange."

There's a scene in Woody Allen's *Take the Money and Run*. He plays the cello in the marching band. Running in formation, carrying his cello in one hand and a chair in the other, he rushes ahead of the band and sets the chair down, drops into the seat and articulates a few notes on the cello, then launches back into step with the band.

I felt like that. Strange, a little absurd.

And I knew what they were thinking. What's this guy going to look like on stage? Blood, Sweat & Tears didn't have a French horn on stage. A trumpet, trombone, and sax made a horn section. Those horns played at the audience. The French horn was a reverse horn, anatomically incorrect. It just didn't match.

They wanted Strecker.

Once Amphagas got going he played a few gigs, but they weren't really a horn band. They were a B-3 band. He graduated from high school and went full-time on his job with the phone company. After a year or two he married Jackie and they moved to Bad Axe.

That fall I played cymbals in the marching band, a matching pair I crashed together with total exuberance. Chicago picked up where Blood, Sweat & Tears left off, releasing "Does Anyone Really Know What Time It Is," a song that leads with a sweet trumpet solo. Jazz rock was a thing.

A WHILE AGO, AFTER trying for a week to fix a haircut, I went back to the salon for take two, a corrective trim.

"Why do you go to her," my daughter asked, "if she cuts your hair crooked?"

Good question.

Besides my wife it's the longest relationship I've had with a woman. Almost thirty years she's cut my hair. It's hands-on work. There's a kind of intimacy, similar to what I feel for my dentist, also a gentle lady, whose nostrils (perfectly symmetrical) I know better than anyone's.

After my shampoo Gemma cuts my hair, and we talk about parents and in-laws, kids and spouses, birthdays and holidays, weddings, vacations, and food. She cuts, she talks. She talks so much sometimes my hair dries before she's finished, which means cold spray in my ears when she squirts me wet again. I can't be sure, but I think she just favors my left shoulder. Would that mean she is right-brain dominant? She stands on my left when she talks. She cuts more on my left.

These days, when she zooms in for the finish with her electric clippers, I give her a little Doug Anderson in the mirror.

"What?" she says.

I don't want to insult her. I point to my right ear. "Just checking."

She stands behind me, pulling the hair above my ears between her thumbs and forefingers.

There's a guy I knew who always tilted his head like this, I could say, cruising down Washington Street in his red Firebird. If his window was down you might hear the radio playing "You've Made Me So Very Happy" or "Brown-Eyed Girl."

"I think it's fine," she says.

I trust her. I tell her I think she's right.

# 7

# Mindful, Bodyful

I HAD ULTERIOR MOTIVES.

For a few years, whenever I had a blood pressure check, as soon as I felt the cuff tighten I waited for the look. Perched on the examination bed at the doctor's office, my arm in the nurse's hand, or on the unforgiving folding chair at the Red Cross donating center, my arm in the nurse's hand, I saw the same look coming as soon as the device began to exhale or once the Velcro patches were ripped apart. Sometimes in midcheck the nurse would tighten the bulb valve and pump me up again just to make sure.

"It's a little high," the nurse would say.

"Yes, but not high-high. Low-high, right?"

"Sometimes just getting blood pressure checked makes a person nervous. The numbers trend higher."

"That's me."

"Do you drink alcohol?"

"Yes."

"How much?"

"Just enough."

My trend was clear. Low-high. And, possibly, getting less low. I promised to watch it. And I did. I was a pretty good spectator, until finally I decided I should become a participant.

Every day for a few weeks I sat down for ten to fifteen minutes in a wing chair in the front room of our house. Sometimes I closed my eyes, sometimes I kept my eyes open. I tried to focus on, well, nothing. Hands resting on my thighs, palms up, palms open! Just breathing. Just concentrating on breaths inhaled and exhaled. Ignoring those little kids wearing bright yellow raincoats (and backpacks! pink and red backpacks) spilling from the bright yellow school bus onto the shiny rain-slicked street. Ignoring Wolf Blitzer droning in the next room, and John Kerry, also droneful, answering Blitzer's questions. Refusing to think about anything, like the inch of oil in Costco-brand natural peanut butter and the maddening task of trying to mix it with that tasty salubrious sludge lying beneath it. Definitely not thinking about that. I had heard Jon Kabat-Zinn talk to Krista Tippett on her radio program "On Being." I had bought his how-to book. I was learning to practice mindfulness. Not that my life up to that time had been mindless, the unhappy implication of the term mindful.

FOR YEARS I HAD suspected that I could become mindful. In 1970, on the ABC Movie of the Week program, I had seen Jan Michael Vincent in the movie "Tribes." He was a pacific suntanned hippy. He had long flowing blond hair and seemed spiritual in a non-denominational way. That could be me, I thought. I wore bellbottoms. If I only could let my hair grow another five to seven inches. Drafted into the Marines, Jan Michael Vincent collides with an immovable object, a drill instructor played by Darren McGavin, who demands obedience and conformity. When Private Archer won't bend Sergeant Drake disciplines him. He forces him to stand in formation and hold aloft two buckets of sand, one in each hand, which Archer does, way past the point of normal human possibility, maintaining a beatific, transcendent look on his face through this whole crucifixion scene. I was moved. It was mind over matter. That could be me, I thought.

Then came college. Transcendental Meditation was a thing. Semester after semester I walked past posters advertising the course. There was a picture of Maharishi Mahesh Yogi. Hey, that was the Beatles' guru. I played the guitar. In my mind the possibility existed, an increasingly remote possibility, I was coming to realize, that I could become if not a Beatle at least Beatlelike. "The Science of Creative Intelligence," the signs said. The course cost ninety dollars.

One night at a party I met Leandra, a girl who had long brown hair and wore sandals and a lot of tie-dye. She had taken the course and described herself as a "devotee."

"Why don't you try it?" she asked.

"Well, you know," I said, "I've got five classes."

"It's not a religion," she said, "if that's what you're worried about."

It wasn't.

"It's just a way of being," she said.

That's what I thought. Being sounded cool. What I wanted to know, I said, was how it worked.

"The nice thing is," she said, "you can do it anywhere." She closed her eyes and held a thoughtful pose for a minute. It looked like she might be slipping into a minimeditation right there, but this wasn't a demo. She was thinking. She shook her head and said she couldn't tell me, I needed to come and find out for myself. (Evidently you signed a nondisclosure agreement when you took the course.) Then she sat down on the floor, crossed her legs, and slid a guitar into her lap. She said she loved Janis Joplin. She began to strum and sing a Janis-esque rendition of "Summertime," a song every beginning guitar player played, milking the soulful A-minor slide. The song went along just fine until she got to that pesky F chord; it required a degree of fingerfulness she had not yet achieved.

We met again at a friend's house a week or so later and drank quite a lot. She prided herself in her ability to drink straight Southern Comfort. I had decided to give Mateus a try, largely because I admired the shape of the bottle. As the night progressed we talked a little more about TM, smoking cigarettes and trading drinks from each other's bottles. I think she was getting close to telling me her mantra when both of us had to call it a night, go home, and throw up.

I kept taking five classes. I kept walking past those posters of the Maharishi.

The rest of my life gradually happened. And gradually meditation and mindfulness lost their countercultural associations.

TODAY MINDFULNESS IS AN industry. It's *in* industry all over the place, from Google to Goldman Sachs to Monsanto. Among its benefits: help with stress, heart disease, chronic pain, high blood pressure; you can improve your sleep, you can deal with substance abuse, with overeating, anxiety, and obsessive-compulsive disorders.

In one of his exercises Kabat-Zinn describes a *New Yorker* cartoon in which two Zen monks in robes and shaved heads, one young, one old, sit side by side cross-legged on the floor. The older one is saying to the younger one, who is turned toward him: "Nothing happens next. This is it." That's the old paradigm. Meditation, Kabat-Zinn writes, "is about not trying to improve yourself or get anywhere else, but simply to realize where you already are."

In the new paradigm and the new delivery system, mindfulness is instrumental. It's results-oriented, prompting the harshest critics to refer to the movement as the "awareness industry," "Yoga-whoring," and the "spiritual-industrial complex."

Sitting in that wing chair, I admit that I was not totally emptying myself of desire. I was meditating to be in the moment, yes, and to be where I already was, but I was also meditating to increase my powers of mind. I wanted results. If Uri Geller could use his mind to bend a spoon, maybe I could use my mind to bend the upward curve of my blood pressure back down into the normal range.

Back in the folding chair, while the Red Cross lady inflated the cuff I focused on my breathing—inhaling, exhaling, believing with all my mind that I could achieve the right number, wanting above all else to continue being glassful, forkful, bodyful.

Then, mindfulness notwithstanding, it would come—the look.

# 8

# Tied

SOMETIME AFTER I STARTED teaching I bought a couple ties designed by Jerry Garcia. They were splashy, artsy-looking things (Jerry Garcia was an art student before he became a legendary guitar player). What was fun was to flip them over and show someone the name on the tag. Jerry Garcia. He makes ties? Then came delight, appreciation. How about that. Which was exactly how I felt.

I'd seen Jerry Garcia the guitar player once, on Sunday, April 4, 1976, in a concert in Page Auditorium at Duke University. If you'd asked me at the time I couldn't have hummed one tune by Jerry Garcia or the Grateful Dead, but he was already a very big deal. I played some guitar. I thought I ought to hear the man play.

Play he did. Not with the Grateful Dead that night, but with the Jerry Garcia Band, which, besides him, was not much of a band. His playing was fluid and melodic and inventive, not the least bit psychedelic. (He and the Dead were famously from San Francisco, so I had kind of expected his play might be, you know, *wild*.) As I remember, the concert was actually kind of boring. I wondered: What was the fuss about?

There's plenty of fuss still, so much that I recently discovered I could go online and find the set list of the concert I saw that night and also find live recordings online of that exact band, on that exact tour, within a few weeks of the concert that night at Duke. When I clicked to play a few of those recordings my reaction was much the same: ho-hum. What stands out in my memory that night, in fact, is not Jerry Garcia. It's the bass player, whose name was John Kahn. He stood next to Garcia, his right hip cocked, a crook in his left knee, all but motionless the whole night, except every so often he would lift his left foot (he was wearing boots), really heft it, about six inches off the ground, probably accepting a good jolt of musical electricity or putting a juicy touch on his bass line. But what it looked like, why I waited for the move, what it looked like was that he had a wad of gum stuck to his boot, and he kept rocking back and pulling up to see if he could get his foot free to take a walk around.

I was wearing one of my Jerry Garcia ties at a colleague's funeral many years after that concert when, slipping away to use the restroom, I looked in a mirror and saw, really saw, my Jerry Garcia tie as if for the first time. On what had appeared to be a splashy, artsy-looking thing, something now suddenly came into focus: a penis. There was a penis on my tie. It was unmistakable. It was a pure Gestalt moment, suddenly seeing an image, in total, for the first time, and being completely unable to unsee it.

I FIRST SAW THE WORD "Gestalt" in the title of a book Jim Williams was reading. Jim was a pal of Dan Timmons. They lived together the summer of 1972 in a rented house on Flajole Road. Dan was riotous. He drank a lot, he smoked a lot of weed, he laughed his head off, he laughed his whole body off, all the time. No one I knew ever had more fun than Dan.

I had run into him that summer at my pre-induction experience, sponsored by the United States Selective Service System. We had both been drafted. At the break between the mental and physical exams, ever the anti-crat, he suggested we go have a drink. "This is Detroit," he said. "There must be a bar nearby." I followed him out of the facility and around the corner to the Bat Lounge, a name that pleased him greatly.

It was four years since the Tet offensive, three years since Woodstock. The United States was well into its long bloody grind to the conclusion of the war. That year 49,514 men were drafted in the

U.S. (a total of 1,857,304 were drafted from August 1964 to February 1973). I ordered a draft beer. He had two whiskies. We talked about our options. I had a doctor's note: busted femurs full of metal. He had a plan, which was to just say no. He was totally confident.

Those summer nights when I arrived at the place on Flajole Road, Dan always said I had just missed the Flajole Road Marimba Band. I don't remember seeing any musical instruments, unless a bong qualifies as an instrument. Many nights, perched on the end of the sofa, Jim sat reading his book about Gestalt therapy. Dan was hilarious; Jim was serious. Dan was in constant motion; Jim was still. Jim had both light and trouble in his pale blue eyes, and concentrated energy. He turned his gaze inward, concentrating on something—on himself, on enlightenment, on his trouble. Whatever it was it absorbed him completely, like a black hole.

"What is it?" I asked him one night.

He nodded, as though he understood the question and he wanted to ponder it.

I waited. He sat there shaking his head.

"Gestalt," I said. "What is it?"

"It's this thing," he said, "about unity."

What unity, I was going to say, but just then Dan started yelling from outside, "Bottle rockets! We got bottle rockets! Let's blow them all up at once!"

I stood up and ran outside, the only sensible course of action. Jim stayed back, thinking.

THE MAN WE SAID goodbye to at that funeral was tall and lanky. He had large hands and a long acquaintance with basketballs. He was an occasional poet, meaning he wrote poetry for occasions. Otherwise, in sensibility, in heart and mind, he was a full-time poet. Years before his death a stroke robbed him of some language capacity. He would speak, and in his speech you would hear the man, his pleasure in language, his beautiful deep voice, his infectious laugh, but when you spoke back to him he would say, first in frustration, then a kind of sorrow, finally with resignation, I can't hear you. He would shake his head, trying to explain. I just can't hear you. As years passed he spent long hours in the backyard, whole summer days polishing Petoskey stones. Every one is a poem, he would say. They were beautiful.

At this funeral one of the eulogists got up and read Edna St. Vincent Millay's poem "Dirge Without Music," a rejection of consolation, a controlled expression of fury at death:

> Gently they go, the beautiful, the tender, the kind;
> Quietly they go, the intelligent, the witty, the brave.
> I know. But I do not approve. And I am not resigned.

I sat there wearing a tie with a penis on it. My colleague would have approved. His eyes would have lit up. Dan Timmons would have laughed his head off. Jim Williams might have managed a mournful smile. And, somewhere, musician and fashion designer Jerry Garcia was playing the guitar and laughing.

# 9

# The Birds and the Beatles

I'M READING A *New Yorker* article about Paul McCartney at the breakfast table. At the top of the page there's a black-and-white photo of him and John Lennon circa 1965. It's the year, the caption tells us, of *Help!* and *Rubber Soul*.

My wife and I are leaving for Italy in a week or so. I've been downloading stuff to my Kindle to read while we're away. I've got enough to last me quite a while, some novels (a few trashy ones, a few edifying ones), Clive James's *Poetry Notebook*, a bunch of articles from the *New Yorker*, the *New York Review of Books*, and the *New Republic*. (I guess I'm keeping it New this spring.) When language fatigue sets in over there, and I know it will, with the constant strain of trying to listen very fast to decode flights of Italian, it's a pleasure to lie down in silence and read in my own language.

"Photo by David Bailey," I say to my wife. Our son's name. "How about that?"

"What?"

"This article about Paul McCartney. It has a photo by David Bailey."

Hmmm.

I give her a minute, then ask, "Who's your favorite Beatle?"

"Don't start."

She's reading a book called *Agents of Empire: Knights, Corsairs, Jesuits and Spies in the Sixteenth-Century Mediterranean World*. The bibliography is forty pages. Good Lord.

"Are you taking that thing on the plane?"

"Maybe." She pushes a small taste of eggs onto her espresso spoon. "It's a brick."

"Jesuits," she says. "I love the Jesuits."

I hum a few bars of "When I'm Sixty-Four." This year two of my pals and I turn sixty-four within a few months of each other. I've suggested more than a few times that we should have a "when I'm sixty-four party" sometime this summer to celebrate ourselves.

LATER THIS DAY I will drive ninety minutes north to visit my old friend Brian. His caretaker Sheila has told me he's not quite himself. It's how she knew something was wrong. Listening to music in the car, piped from my iPhone into the radio, I make a mental note of oldies I'd like to play for him. "I've Got Friday on My Mind," by the Easybeats. Cyrcle's "It's a Turn Down Day." The Beatles' "Dr. Robert," so we can hear that scratchy guitar and lush chorus. I'd like to see him react to the organ solo in Bonnie Raitt's "We Used to Rule the World." In the car I play the music loud, today even louder than usual. I know I probably shouldn't. My wife and kids tell me I'm getting a little deaf. (A little?) These days the car and treadmill are the only places I listen to music. I can't help myself. I want it loud.

He'll be sitting in his wheelchair at the kitchen table, his back to the doorway I walk through. I rehearse the scene in my mind. "Remember this?" Sitting across from him I'll play part of a song. I'll wait to see the look of recognition, watch him travel back in time. "How about this?"

When my mother was sick and I made this drive, I listened to podcasts, for reflection and for laughs. For these visits I want bang and bash. I want nostalgia.

WE BOUGHT EVERY BEATLES album as soon as it hit the store. This was, of course, back in the vinyl days. The first three or four LPs, in mono, cost less than five dollars. We took them home, put them on the turntable, and sat down to listen. It was "close listening," almost like the close reading of a poem advocated by the New Critics. In the front bedroom of Brian's house on Third Street we sat on the floor and played the records over and over, holding the album covers, like holy objects, in our laps. There was a photo or two to look at; on the back, a song list. You listened and you looked. "Meet the Beatles," headshots of four young guys in partial shadow; twelve songs, the longest of which was "I Saw Her Standing There" (2:50), the shortest, incredibly short by today's standards, "Little Child" (1:46), produced by George Martin for Capitol Records.

Years later my kids went totally digital. They bought CDs and queued up the songs they wanted to hear. On some CDs they listened to only one or two songs; that was it. Back in the vinyl days we listened to the whole album, every track all the way through, even the songs we didn't particularly like. Ringo singing "Act Naturally." Really? To lift the needle, move it to the song you liked, and set it down, aiming for the barely visible gap between tracks, was to risk scratching the record.

A scratch would last forever. That was the thing about vinyl.

And now it's back.

I have purist friends who could explain why vinyl is better: the sound profiles you get in analog are richer, far superior to the sterile precision of digital. I guess I get that. I'm still kind of an analog guy. I look at the clock and say "a quarter to" and "a little after"; it bothers me that soon kids will no longer be able to decode the face of a clock and tell time, the way many of them will never learn to write in cursive. I remember tuning in stations on the AM radio in the car. Even today I like a speedometer *needle*. I go *about* seventy miles per hour (not sixty-seven) when I drive up to visit Brian.

I should ask him, What do you think about the vinyl craze these days?

I know what he would say.

Who gives a damn?

HE'S SITTING IN HIS wheelchair with his back to the door. The dogs bark when I walk in. There are seven of them. It takes a minute to calm them down. Brian gives me a crooked smile and says, "How the hell are you?" It's his usual greeting. He has a full beard, a lot more salt than pepper, and he's wearing a hat. It occurs to me that in all the recent pictures of him I've seen he has that hat on. When I ask him how the hell *he's* doing, he turns his head and points to his hair, slate gray, wisps of what's left of it hanging down. It's the radiation, he says.

I figure we'll get a few basics out of the way before getting down to basics.

Sleep?

He says he sleeps just fine.

Appetite?

He says he's an eating machine.

Pain?

Not even a headache. If the doctor didn't tell him he was sick he wouldn't even know it.

I ask if he's ever had a beard before.

Couple times.

He's sixty-four years old, a September birthday, a year older than I am. Three months ago Sheila organized a benefit. It went from noon to nine at the Elks Club bar in Bay City, all music all the time, played by over forty years of musician friends in the area. Brian packed the place.

I tell him I'm thinking about a "when I'm sixty-four party" for me and a few pals this summer. What does he think?

Yup.

Next to the kitchen table a TV set displays weekday afternoon programming. He watches it while I ask more questions, about his sister, son, nephew, a pal we call Easy Eddie. I'm thinking about my song list when he wonders, Hey, what're we going to eat?

IN THIS *NEW YORKER* article, published in 2007, Paul McCartney confesses to dyeing his hair. He also confesses to being freaked out about actually being sixty-four. "The thought is somewhat horrifying," he tells the interviewer. "It's like 'Well, no, this can't be me.'" The article is contemporaneous with the release of an album called "Memory Almost Full," which the interviewer describes as "up-tempo rock songs . . . tinged with melancholy." I know the album. When it came out I listened to thirty seconds of each track at the iTunes Store, bought one song, "Dance Tonight," for $1.29, and downloaded it. It's a jaunty piece with a kazoo solo in the bridge.

The writer mentions the famous deaths: Lennon, Harrison, Linda.

McCartney, I learn, was sixteen when he wrote "When I'm Sixty-Four."

When Brian and I were that age we had begun to realize we were not going to be the next Lennon and McCartney. We had written exactly one song together, called "If I Could Dream," which some years later he managed to get recorded with a band he was in, graciously crediting "Bailey and Bennett" in parentheses beneath the song title as the composers.

I COME BACK FROM Mulligans with two bar burgers, mushrooms and mayo on his, and French fries. The dogs bark. Four or five of them eventually settle under the table. We eat our burgers and watch a little more TV, and I think again about my song list. Maybe I won't play the songs after all. Who wants to listen to music on a phone anyway? In the kitchen it will sound like a cheap transistor radio.

I say, "Hey, remember 'It's a Turn Down Day'?"

He looks at the TV for a bit, then turns my way. "The Cyrcle," he says. "They were a good band."

The show we're watching is called *The Doctor*. It's talk. Two men, two women. One of the men is dressed like a doctor. They're discussing castration as a way of punishing rapists. Or maybe it's a preventative measure. The man dressed as a doctor explains that there are both surgical and chemical castration. The two women agree that, either way, it's an extreme measure. They are both against it.

I try another one: "Remember 'I've Got Friday on My Mind'?"

It takes a minute. He turns away from the TV and gives me a partial crooked smile and a nod. "Good song," he says.

I know the nod.

Sheila says, "Getting tired, Brian?"

It's for me. Well, okay, I think, that's enough.

We sit together for a while longer, through the rest of my fries. Brian takes a bite or two from his burger, gazes at the TV. Before going to commercial the doctor previews the next segment of the show. They're going to talk about a woman's cancer treatment. The woman on screen looks familiar.

"Is that Bruce Jenner?" I say.

Sheila says it's not Bruce Jenner. It's a real woman.

"Goddam," Brian says.

We watch a few more minutes in silence. I get up to go. The dogs rouse and congregate around my feet. I tell Brian see you in a month or so, shake his hand, and lean down for a long hug. "You hang in there now," I say. "I'll be back the middle of next month."

He nods, says thanks for coming, Richard.

"See you, right?"

He nods. I'm pretty sure he nods.

About the time I get to the freeway, which takes ten minutes or so, my iPhone shuffles to a favorite Beatles song. I play it loud and sing along: "You say you've seen certain wonders, and your bird can sing." That would be another song to mention, on another visit.

A FEW DAYS LATER my wife and I are upstairs packing. It's mid-morning. I'm tossing power cords for my phone and Kindle and laptop into a carry-on when I realize I'm not wearing any pants. What happened to my pants?

"Have you seen my black sweater?" my wife says.

When did I take off my pants? For a while now I've been walking into rooms only to find I can't remember why I'm there. I'm used to that. Like tinnitus, it comes with age. Losing my pants is new.

"Did you hear me?" my wife says.

"I heard you." I look around the room, feeling mild panic. No pants anywhere. "Which black sweater?"

I stand there marveling at this altered state. Then I remember: I took them off in the other room, in front of the closet, so I could try on another pair I had fitted a while back.

"I'm losing it," she says.

There they are, the pants I tried on, in the carry-on. So the other ones are over there?

"Can you hear anything I'm saying?" she says.

"I hear you fine."

We're all losing it.

One of these days I'll have to get my hearing checked. I sort of don't want to know. I think about my parents growing old, my father and all his hearing aids. There were owls in the woods a half a mile away from their house. My parents almost always slept with a window open. For years they said they heard owls all night. One day my wife and I were up for a visit. When I asked about them, my mother said yes, the owls were still there. Then she added, "Your dad can't hear them anymore." I think he took it in stride. What choice did he have? Still, it broke my heart.

One day it will happen to me. I'll wake up, look for my pants, and I won't be able to hear the birds and the Beatles. I'll have to remember to consider myself lucky.

# 10

# Cookies and What?

COWS, I LEARNED RECENTLY, can't walk down stairs. The problem is weight distribution and the way their knees bend. So you can invite them up, but you may be asking for trouble.

I've been thinking a lot about cows and milk ever since the holistic doctor I see told me to cut milk from my diet. I don't see him because I'm sick. I see him because I want to be more well. He's my age, thin and energetic, an MD who realized the limits of traditional medicine early in his career and went alternative. Once a year I get blood work and see him. He checks all my levels and suggests dietary adjustments and supplements. I didn't know it, but I'm low on iodine. I need a little more selenium in my life. More vitamin C and D. The store is in the front of the office. They take credit cards.

"Casein," he says one day. We're in the examination room. On the wall is an acupuncture chart. "You're allergic to casein."

I tell him I feel fine.

I've always been a firm believer in milk. My parents told me to drink my milk. The TV told me it's a natural. It does a body good. Got milk? Yup. When lactose intolerance became a thing I sniffed at it as a fad and embraced milk like never before.

"I don't object to cheese," he says, "but I'd like you to try to cut milk from your diet."

I don't sneeze. I don't have a runny nose. I don't have rash or hives. How can I be allergic?

"Inflammation," he says. "Gut." He shows me all my levels in the blood work. Next to each value is normal range. He points to casein. Milkwise I'm above normal.

He tells me I'll feel better.

"I feel good."

He taps the blood work printout. "Try it."

"What about cappuccino?"

"Try a milk substitute."

"There is no substitute."

He says I'll probably lose weight.

I communed with cows, you might say, when I was a kid. My grandfather, a rural mail carrier, had a small farm. He milked eight cows every morning and every night. He called them, *Cu boossss!* at dusk, and they came to the barn, slowly, with soulful, cowful grace. Once they took their stalls he pulled a stool next to them and milked them. The sweet smell of hay mixed with cow piss, their lifted tails and prodigious plops of dung, the sound of their steady jets of milk hitting the pail: these are foundational memories for me.

When there was a calf the grandkids got to name it. My calf was Hester, a name suggested by my mother. My brother named his calf Sheep. He thought of that on his own. When the calves pushed their noses through the fence in the barn, we stuck our fingers in their mouths to feel their slimy tongues and eager sucking search for udders. It was mysterious. And terrifying.

"Try it," I said to my kids years later. We were in Romeo one fall, a small town north of Detroit, on a pumpkin buy, when we stopped at the petting zoo. There were goats, rabbits, ducks, and a couple calves. The calves nosed through the fence in our direction. I held out two fingers, inserted them, felt the strong gooey suck.

"No way," my daughter said.

My son took a step closer to his mother.

THE THING IS, FOR cappuccino, I've recently started using the hard stuff—whole milk. Skim or 1 percent, don't waste your time. Yes, the milk foams, it shapeshifts into huge billowy, frothy clouds, but there's no density. Ever been on an airplane descending through a cloud? That's lowering your face to skim and 1 percent foam. White nothingness. For the longest time I believed in 2 percent, which produces a substantial froth and warm, full-bodied milk to stain your coffee. Then just recently I went whole, and I was home.

IT'S TRUE MILK WILL mess with you. I know from experience.

When our daughter was two years old we brought her to Italy for the first time. It was August. It was hot. Our first days we went straight to the beach on the Adriatic. She wore a hat, we slathered sunscreen all over her, we stayed out of the sun in the afternoon. We kept her under the umbrella when she played with her cousins in the sand. At regular intervals she took milk from a bottle, her preferred delivery system. The third day she was listless. She had developed a moving rash. We called a doctor friend of the family. He came to our apartment and looked at her belly.

"Maybe there was something in the sand," my wife said.

"Maybe," he said.

"I think she got too much sun," an aunt said.

"Possibly," he said.

"She should have some broth," my mother-in-law said, her prescription for any ailment.

"Always a good idea," the doctor agreed.

"I think it's the milk," I said. They were all speaking Italian. Nobody heard me.

"Bring me a soup spoon," the doctor said to my mother-in-law. He turned to my wife. "The rash is probably orticaria."

"What did he say?" I asked.

"He said it's orticaria."

"What's that?" I asked

"What's that?" she asked.

"It's a rash," the doctor told her.

My mother-in-law came back with the soup spoon, which he

took from her and said, in Italian, that he needed to see our daughter's throat. He wasted no time on negotiation. He pried her mouth open with the spoon, looked at her throat, and withdrew the spoon.

"There's nothing to do," he said. "You'll have to wait."

Meantime the baby wailed.

Over the next week or so the rash migrated from her arms to her legs, from her stomach to her back. It was a moving target. We dusted her with baking soda. She stopped eating. She spiked a fever. She didn't eat for three days. One night, after refusing the broth pushed at her, she agreed to eat a hot dog, an American food she could reason with. All along she had been drinking what struck me as an odd form of milk, a Parmalat product that sat on shelves unrefrigerated, capable of maintaining through months of storage, thicker than the milk she was accustomed to. It was strong. It tasted bad in coffee.

"I think it's the milk," I said to my wife one night. The baby slept in her lap, a hot rashy mess.

"Or the sand. Or the heat."

"But that milk," I said. "Have you tasted it?"

Next day the aunt brought down some fresh milk in a half-liter carton. It was cool, the right consistency. It was clearly and unmistakably the milk we knew. Our daughter got better.

I know. *Post hoc ergo propter hoc.* After this, therefore because of this. Maybe the orticaria just ran its course. Still, she got better. And the coffee tasted good.

MY EFFORT TO QUIT milk is less than valiant.

For a few weeks I try soy milk. I find I can drink the stuff. I can even enjoy it as long as I don't put it in coffee; it ruins coffee. Forget trying to froth it. All I can get it to do is bubble. Who wants hot bubbles in their coffee? And sorry, but soy milk is the wrong color. Is it good for me? A casual search for the health benefits of drinking soy milk produces contradictory results. Here's the truth from a bunch of websites: Fitday, the six benefits of soy milk; Empowered Sustenance, ten reasons to never drink soy milk; Authority Nutrition, Is soy bad for you? The shocking truth; Health Fitness Revolution, Health benefits of soy milk; Natural Health Newsletter, Benefits of soy and soy protein danger.

The Harvard School of Public Health, in "Straight Talk about Soy," reports that evidence of benefits is inconclusive.

Worst of all, soy milk is only good *by itself.* Cookies and soy milk? No thanks. Apple pie and a glass of soy milk? I'll pass.

Next I try almond milk. It flunks a series of tests.

Rice milk, ditto.

There are milks galore: goat milk, sheep milk, camel milk, hemp milk, coconut milk, hazelnut milk, oat milk, cashew milk, flax milk—each, I'm sure, with its salubrious qualities. How hard do we want to work at this?

One morning I'm at my daughter's house. She's a mom now, with a kid about the age she was when orticaria took her by storm. She pours me coffee, opens the fridge, and takes out a half gallon of organic, ultrapasteurized 2 percent milk with DHA Omega-3 added.

"What's DHA Omega-3?"

"I don't know," she says. "I think it's supposed to be good for you."

"I bet it is." When I check later that day I find totally contradictory claims. It's an elixir; it's poison.

"It was all they had on the shelf last night," she says.

"As long as it's good in coffee." I pour some in my cup and taste. Welcome home.

# 11

# GelatiAmo

"THEY NEVER HAVE YOUR FAVORITE," I say to my wife.

She's lying on the sofa reading a book entitled *Pagans: The End of Traditional Religion and the Rise of Christianity*. Usually when she reads she pauses and gives me updates, sometimes lengthy ones. With this book, however, her glosses have been terse. Yesterday when I asked what was happening she said simply, "Cicero."

"Flavor," I say now. I mean favorite gelato flavor.

We've just come from a sprawling Italian market in Shelby Township called Vince and Joe's, where we stood a full fifteen minutes in front of the gelato case and she looked and looked and, well, *pined* just a little. She said the sight of all that gelato made her homesick. She chose three flavors, three pints: café, pistachio, and nutella. They're in the freezer right now, getting frozen.

I tell her I found something she might be interested in.

She sets her book aside, finally.

"In Riccione," a town on the Adriatic a half hour from her village in San Marino, "a festival," I say, "dedicated to gelato. It's called GelatiAmo." When I tell her it's written all one word, with that odd Capital A (the term is a play on words, making "gelato" into a verb, meaning roughly "Let's gelato!" or "I love gelato"), she squints, as if picturing the word, smiles a little, and turns back to her book.

I HAVE A DEFECTIVE sweet tooth. Unlike my wife I am only *mildly* crazy about gelato.

I first glimpsed the larger possibilities of ice cream when I was in college. There was a Baskin-Robbins on the edge of campus (for some reason, I called it Baskin *and* Robbins). Up until then, for me ice cream was something you bought by the half gallon, either vanilla or chocolate, at the supermarket. Occasionally my mother got a little wild and went black walnut on us. But for the most part our family stuck to the two bedrock flavors.

Thursday nights after class my junior year I began stopping for ice cream. I gravitated to French vanilla. So many choices, though. On any given night you would find a variety of chewy, rich, dairy-fat sugar bombs, flavors (the word hardly seems apt) like Bananas Foster, Cherries Jubilee, Chocolate Chip Cookie Dough, Cotton Candy, Made with Snickers, Mom's Making Cookies, and Reese's Peanut Butter Cup. In their cardboard buckets they looked like ice creams, but to me a flavor like Caramel Praline Cheesecake just sounded like a grotesque mistake.

The Thursday night ice cream girl behind the counter had a round face and short, blond milkmaid hair. She smiled at me as she handed me the miniature purple plastic tasting spoons. I tried to make conversation.

"So how long have you worked at Baskin and Robbins?"

"Baskin-Robbins," she said. "There's no 'and.'"

"Is it cold back there?"

"Kinda."

"Have you tried all these?"

"No."

"Which one do you like?"

"Rocky Road."

"Do your arms get tired, you know, scooping?"

"Sometimes."

I sensed we were slowly moving in the right direction. One night I thought I would show her I was capable of being adventurous. I said I'd like to taste Ambrosia.

"That's new, isn't it?"

"Yes."

"What's in it?"

She handed me the little spoon and said she didn't know.

I tasted it. "Ambrosia," I said, "nectar of the gods."

"There's only one God," she answered.

Well, never mind. I said I liked it and asked for two scoops just to make a point.

I HAD MY FIRST gelato a few months after I got married. My wife took me back to Italy. A few blocks down the street from her Aunt Angela's was the *lungomare*, Rimini's segment of the Adriatic Riviera, an almost continuous strip of beaches and umbrellas, hotels and *pensione*, bars and discotheques, restaurants and *gelaterie* extending from Ravenna south to Fano and beyond. Back then the newest and greatest gelato was made by Nuovo Fiore.

The old Zia was a terrific cook, an encyclopedia of gluttonous delights she had learned from the nuns she lived with in cloister when she was a schoolgirl. One night, after sea snails and clams and a handmade pasta called *strozzopreti* (priest chokers), we walked down Via Pascoli, crossed the railroad tracks, and came to Nuovo Fiore, a gleaming establishment on the corner. No cardboard buckets. There were shiny stainless-steel basins of velvety gelati, a riot of bright colors, labels above each flavor with names like *mirtilli, fragola, mora, liquirizia, nocciola*, and *stracciatella*. We tasted a number of *gusti* with small purple plastic tasting spoons. Gelato, I discovered, was softer than ice cream, smoother, not as cold. Delicious.

My wife elbowed me. "What do you want?"

"A small cup," I said. "*Crema*."

"That's vanilla," she said. "Really?"

"Okay, I'll try one of the chocolates."

"Let me order for you."

She did. I don't remember what flavor I tried that night. What I do recall is *panna montata*, a small, weightless swirl of whipped cream resting on top of the gelato. The gelato was good, *really* good. The panna was heaven. We were in Italy seven days. We had gelato every day, sometimes twice.

THE FAT'S THE THING, and air, and temperature, that makes gelato, and makes it different from ice cream. Gelato has less butterfat than ice cream, 4–9 percent as opposed to 15–25 percent. Gelato is churned more slowly, which means less air is worked into it, yielding greater density. And gelato is served at a warmer temperature than ice cream. (Note to self: Take the gelato out of the freezer fifteen minutes before we want to eat it.) You get a creamy, silky structure you can plunge a spoon into; on your tongue and palate it melts and spreads out. And there is flavor.

Flavor? I honestly don't know that gelato *tastes* better than ice cream. (Of course it does, my wife would say.) It's just different. It *feels* different in your mouth. Also, while you're eating it, if you're lucky, there's the sea over there, or a piazza, or a cathedral and bell tower. Never underestimate the impact of place on taste.

Occasionally I follow my wife to new flavors—*fichismo* (fresh ricotta with caramelized figs) or *pesca al forno* (baked peaches with chocolate and amaretti)—but I tend to default to vanilla and chocolate. Boring, she says. *Crema, nutella, nocciola, gianduia, bacio*—that's boring I can live with.

Whereas her favorite gelato is *zuppa inglese*, the Italian version of English trifle: a dessert of sponge cake soaked in cherry liquor with layers of custard and chocolate. She would go back to Orvieto any day, not to see the magnificent duomo again so much as to revisit the gelateria right next to the cathedral where she remembers the best zuppa inglese gelato she's ever had. There are varieties of religious experience.

Gelato, to paraphrase James Joyce, is general all over Italy. When we hit a new town over there and feel the need, we ask two or three people where the best gelato is. Usually the response is immediate. There's the smile, the widening eyes, the look of rapture.

Life is short. Don't forget to gelato.

# 12

# Beheading

IN THE SHOWER ONE morning, against my will, I find myself humming "I've Had the Time of My Life." Through most of my marriage I've thought the guy singer was Michael Bolton, but when I heard it in the car the other day, when I really *heard* the song, I knew it had to be a Righteous Brother, the tall one. Now I'm stuck with this song in my head.

I squirt a glob of shampoo into my hand, trying to sing Bill Medley low, and begin to suds up my head. In the seventh grade, long before Michael Bolton, when both Righteous Brothers sang "You've Lost That Lovin' Feeling," I slow-danced with Judy Schilling to that song at lunchtime. Since then there's been a lot of lovin' feeling lost and gained.

Later, when I come downstairs, I ask my wife which Righteous Brother she liked best, the big one or the little one.

She's reading Umberto Eco at the breakfast table. After all these years of marriage she's learned to ignore such questions. "Eco is talking about the casting of *Perseus*," she says without looking up. "It's Cellini, isn't it?"

I fill a coffee cup for myself. "Is there a Donatello *Perseus*?"

She shakes her head. "You're thinking of *Judith and Holofernes*," she says. "A different beheading altogether."

Actually I'm still thinking about the Righteous Brothers.

She reads, I fix myself cereal and sit across the table from her, googling Western civilization. I decide to look for Donatello's *Perseus*. She's right, of course.

"So which one?" I ask her again. I stare across the table at her until she has to stop reading and look up. I'm having the time of my life.

"Cellini's the *Perseus*. It says so right here in the Eco. But I knew it."

"Big or little?"

She closes the book, takes a drink of coffee, and looks at me. "What are you talking about?"

"The Righteous Brothers," I say.

"Neither," she says. "You knew that."

"One of them died," I say.

"I'm sorry to hear that," she says. And that settles it.

She returns to her book, turns a page, says quietly that she loves Eco. Just loves him. When she asks I fix her another cappuccino. Later I'll make her breakfast, thinking about a Righteous Brother lost.

# 13

# Idaho

MY FRIEND O.R. IS coming to town. First time I've seen him in twenty-some years. And he's bringing with him this Trish he's been talking about. On the phone he calls her his not-quite wife.

"What's the O.R. again?" my wife says.

Odell Robert.

"And what's he coming for?"

"An ice sculpture show," I say. "He's learning the art of ice."

O.R. and I, we go way back. He would take a pounding from his dad, a big disgruntled man who wore cowboy boots and built TV sets in his basement. His old man had a short temper that lasted a long time. We would escape to the edge of our wide, slow-moving river that smelled bad and never froze. Sitting on a culvert that leaked runoff into the river, we drank Royal Crown Cola and belched the names of places we wanted to visit when we got older, when we finally made our exit. Names rich in vowels led us to freedom and adventure. Ohio, Iowa, Oklahoma. Utah. Cities too. O.R. perfected an interrogative belch. "Omaha?" he'd go. "Albuquerque," I would declare. Some days we crossed the Pacific. "Hawaii?" he'd ask. "Oahu," I'd belch in reply.

Today he's coming home from Wyoming.

We meet at a roadhouse outside town. He wheels a long yellow Buick into the lot. It's low, rusty, and full of Lynyrd Skynyrd. The guy that drags himself out of the car is big, wears cowboy boots, and pounds me hello on the back.

"You pissant," he says. "You never did escape."

When I introduce my wife she disappears into his chest in his giant hug. Trish is blond, thin, with nervous fingers that tap Morse code through introductions and the first pitcher we drink. O.R. and I catch up. His parents, dead. Mine, not. His sisters, alive— all four of them mothers, divorced or widowed, becoming ladies of the Lord.

"You?" he says.

"Holy moly," I belch. That gets us started. We revisit old destinations while the girls talk. Another pitcher, then another. O.R. leaves the table, comes back. A few minutes later, when he leaves the table again, I turn to Trish.

"So," I say. "Ice?"

"Trish says she wants to be a masseuse," my wife says.

Trish examines her hands and nods. "Odell says I got hot hands."

She raises one to her forehead and this melting happens. *Oh no,* I think. *She's going to cry.*

"You know what he's doing in there," she says. "You know why he keeps going to the bathroom."

I say, "No, but I can guess."

She taps the end of her nose. "There's no ice sculpture," she says. "We sorta had to run away from Wyoming." She drags a french fry through a puddle of catsup, picks it up, and drops it.

"She tell you about her hot hands?" O.R. says when he comes back. He drinks down the last of his beer. "Goddam right," he says.

A month or so later Trish calls. They're back in Wyoming. O.R.'ll have some jail time to do. She's taking a course. A good masseuse, she tells me, can make a decent living.

That night I lie in bed with my wife imagining O.R., my old friend, in a cell. Concrete walls. Cold, I think, but the acoustics might echo pretty good. Where will he go next? Idaho? Arizona? There's no end of places.

# 14

# Good Bad

"AREN'T YOU GOING TO eat that thing?" my wife says.

We're on I-80 eastbound, halfway across Pennsylvania. It's midafternoon. On the console between the two front seats in the car, in a paper bag, is a McDonald's hamburger. It's the third time we've made this trip by car to visit our son in New York. At seventy-seven miles per hour, with one stop for gas, construction slow-downs, and horrible Newark, the drive from Detroit to Manhattan takes ten hours.

On long interstate trips like this, food is a problem. We leave around seven o'clock in the morning. Too early to stop for Arabic takeout. It's just as well. I would probably have tahini dribbles up and down my shirt. One trip, the morning we left, we bought "summer sandwiches" from a purveyor of designer food in our area. Slices of fresh mozzarella on French bread; the "summer" ingredients were tomato and basil. By the time we got to the sandwiches that afternoon the bread was leathery and bite-resistant. Think jerky. Our recent do-it-yourself solution is chicken strips we grill the night before and roll up in romaine leaves the next day. It's a bite-friendly snack; a little protein, a little summer; moderate-to-low dribble risk. This trip we didn't think ahead.

We're coming up on the Clearfield exit when I turn to my wife and suggest we stop at the next exit for gas.

"Fine," she says.

"Get out and stretch your legs," I say. "Are you hungry?"

"Yes," she says. "But I won't eat."

"I'm going to get one McDonald's hamburger," I announce. A few miles back I saw the sign, the arches, the big M.

She frowns across the dash, shakes her head.

"It's the perfect food," I say.

"I read somewhere that adults who eat fast food are stuck in their adolescence."

I like to make pinpoint visits to that confusing time of life. "I remember eating a McDonald's hamburger when I was a kid," I say. "All in one bite. It was the summer I graduated from high school. I thought, Can I do it? The answer was, Yes! But it took a long time. You can get a whole hamburger in your mouth. The problem is what to do with it once it's in there."

"Stop."

"Because you can't chew."

"Please, stop."

"Your mouth is so full, chewing is out of the question. You just wait for it to, you know, soften. Your natural juices have that effect. It gradually gets a little mushy, starts to disintegrate. After a few minutes you can massage it inside your mouth."

She says, "I don't suppose there will be any good food at this exit."

"It took about five minutes or so to eat it."

She says, "Someplace that has fresh vegetables. Is that too much to ask?"

It's definitely too much to ask. I take the exit, thinking first McDonald's, then gas.

I admit to her it's gross. Your mouth full of a whole hamburger; it's like a snake eating a mouse. I have the decency to keep this thought to myself.

There's one girl behind the counter in McDonald's, taking orders. She has blades of brown hair swept to the right across her broad forehead, a bored look on her round face. At the end of every order she hands over a receipt, announces the order number, and tells the customer to have an amazing day. In the olden days she would then turn, grab your food, bag it, and you would be on your way. It was fast. In the new Macs there's a fulfillment station at the other end of the counter. Division of labor, I guess. Plus there are all those healthy choices on the menu. Those foods take time. I'm number ninety-seven, for coffee and the standard-issue hamburger. I have to wait for someone's Premium Southwest Salad with Crispy Chicken and Angus Mushroom & Swiss Snack Wrap to be fulfilled.

But then something wonderful happens.

While I stand there waiting the fulfillment lady comes to the counter holding two ice cream cones. "Who wants a free ice cream cone?" she says brightly. I look around. Behind me a guy is holding his little girl. She lurches forward in his arms and reaches for the ice cream cones with both hands. In front of me a couple women, I'm thinking early octogenarians, both with gray hair and sturdy legs, swing around and glance at me. They smile and nod at the little girl, encouraging her. I swear they smile and nod at me too, giving me permission.

"Yes!" I say.

Oh, God, yes. It's vanilla. Sweet and creamy and delicious. I've licked it down halfway by the time I get my food and step outside.

"Free ice cream," I say to my wife. She's standing by her car door.

"That's not ice cream," she says.

"I know," I say. "And it's amazing."

She points across the street, where there's a Dutch Pantry. "I could have gone over there," she says, "and got something to go."

I tell her she still can. I have to pump gas. Down the road is a Mobil and an Arby's. Beyond that, a Sunoco and a Snappy's.

"Want to try the Snappy's?" I say. "Make it Snappy?"

She rolls her eyes. She just can't bring herself to eat bad food, which I understand, but there is such a thing as good bad food. I've gone the good bad route.

In a few minutes we're back on I-80, doing seventy-seven miles per hour, and I'm remembering the summer after high school graduation. I told my father one night I was thinking about moving to New York. You mean City? he said, aghast. Yes, New York City.

When he pointed out, didn't I think I should go to college first, a major part of his plan for me over the past eighteen years, I told him I really thought I should give New York a try. I needed to find out. I played the guitar. I had written one song. My only other talents were that I was good at algebra and could eat a McDonald's hamburger in one bite. Did I know anyone in New York? No. How was I planning on getting there? I didn't know. Hitchhike, I guess? He saw the city, I'm sure, in black and white—filth, profanity, violence, and death—well, all black; while I saw it in a whitish blur, with me in it, growing my hair a little longer, playing the guitar, getting to work writing another song, deep in a process of self-discovery. Let's think about it, my father said. A month later my one-song cowriter friend and I drove to Louisville in his blue vw, listening to Blind Faith on his eight-track tape deck. We were going to meet with a record producer my friend said he sort of knew down there. We checked into a Holiday Inn when we hit town. My friend, I discovered, had not thought about how we would contact this producer on a Saturday night. I don't think he even had a phone number. I was actually kind of relieved. Later that night, at a party store near the hotel, we asked someone in the parking lot to buy us some beer. At least the trip wasn't a total bust.

"Aren't you going to eat that thing?" my wife says.

We're starting to see signs for the Poconos. I don't know if I can bring myself to eat the hamburger. The ice cream has taken the edge off my appetite. But, also, I don't want to eat it in front of her while she goes hungry. I feel kind of guilty. Maybe Dutch Pantry had fresh vegetables or vegetables that used to be fresh. We should have checked.

"Probably not," I say.

"What are you going to do with it?"

I tell her I might give it to a homeless person when we get to New York. Yes, what I'll do is drop my wife off at our son's apartment, park the car down on Lafayette and Great Jones, then walk up Broadway to Eleventh Street. There might be someone down and out lying in the shadows along the way. Here you go, man. In Chicago once my wife went into a Panera and bought a homeless person a sandwich. Panera. It seemed like overkill.

"What homeless person would want a cold McDonald's hamburger?" she says.

"If I were homeless, I would love one," I say. "Absolutely."

I know it's childish, but it irks me that she has insulted my hamburger.

"It's good," I say, "even cold."

We cruise in silence for a while, scanning FM, looking without success for National Public Radio. At the Delaware Cut my appetite returns. I think, *What the hell*. I reach in the bag, unwrap the hamburger, and take a bite. It's cold. It's bad, I know it's bad, but it's so good. The soft, yeasty bun; the flat, fatty, beef-like patty; the sweet rejoinder of ketchup; two vivid dill pickle slices; and when I take a second bite a spray of diced onions, like unpolished diamonds, a few of which fall in my lap.

"We'll have good food tonight," my wife says, "in New York."

"There are no guarantees," I say. Prior trips we've had plenty of bad good food.

I take another small bite. I could eat the rest of it all at once. For old time's sake I could stuff it. But I know now it's too good for that. I want to savor it. Even this lowly burger, it's good. Besides, I am an adult.

# 15

# Critters

"WOULDN'T YOU KNOW IT," my wife says.

We pull up to a red light a mile from our house. It's seven in the morning. Stopped in front of us is a pest control truck. On the back of it, facing us, is the company name, telephone number, and an all-star list of domestic pests that, if you don't watch it, can get out of control. Wasps, ants, termites, bats, raccoons, ground hogs, mice—each pictured with a larger-than-life-size photo for the reading-impaired or animal-challenged, or both, on the back of the truck.

"They're getting an early start today," I say. My wife averts her gaze. It's the mouse, I know, that she can't look at. "Or maybe last night was a stakeout."

I lean toward her, lift and check my face in the rear-view mirror. I have a pimple on my nose, in the early stages of formation. It's just to the left of the septum, getting big and red and tender.

I ask her how noticeable it is. Just in passing, you know, can you see it. I'm giving a talk in a few days to a small group, anticipating the feedback at the end of the session. *Nice presentation. Does that thing hurt?*

"It's barely visible," she says.

"But you can see it."

"I'm not looking."

"I mean if you glanced in my direction."

"Yes, sort of visible. Stop."

I knew girls when I was in high school, I tell her, who would stay home when they got a pimple. One of those big ones that erupt and get kind of crusty. Sometimes they went into seclusion for a couple days.

The pest control truck completes a right turn. My wife says maybe we should call them. Or someone.

This summer we are overrun with pests.

My wife distinguishes between good and bad pests. Fireflies are on the rise. Good. Then there are spiders, a year-round pest, also, depending on whom you talk to, good. She forbids me to kill a spider. They eat bad bugs, she says, without specifying which. Any time of year, lying in bed, when we see a spider stuck to the ceiling or wall, honoring her wishes I climb up on a chair and delicately extract it, cradling it between thumb and forefinger in a tissue, then carry it downstairs, open the front door, and, any time of year, throw it out of the house on its ear.

"Did you kill it?" she'll ask.

"I don't think so. It might have bumped its head."

Then there are up-and-coming pests.

Earwigs, for example, are everywhere. It's the indoor-outdoor pest. Down at the end of the driveway a colony of them lives in our mailbox. They run to the back of the box when you swing open the little door. To be safe we try to remember to fan the mail out and shake it before bringing it in the house, before reading it.

We have ants in the yard. No surprise. If you mow you know. But there are more of them in the last couple years. My wife, gardening around the yard, discovered them the other day and alerted me.

"Shouldn't we do something?" she says.

"What?"

"You saw what they did to the brick walk."

There's a depression, an area just off the porch, where the paving stones have sort of sunk. I roll the gas grill on top of it so I don't have to think about it, so she doesn't have to see the concavity. I tell her I think that was chipmunks, a pest, like spiders, she happens to like.

"There's a bald spot on the lawn," she says. We walk outside and stand over a round, receding grassline. The turf, what's left of it, is raised. "What do you think they're up to?"

I tell her it's a mystery. And it is: so much of the natural world, going about its business as if we weren't even here, will startle us suddenly, get our attention when it gets too close, as when critters wish to cohabitate. Where did earwigs come from? I never saw them when I was a kid. Now they're everywhere. Along with Canada geese. And groundhogs. These pests were out there all along, somewhere in nature. Just somewhere else. Now they're here in large quantities.

My policy is to leave them alone. As long as they're not in the house I give them carte blanche.

"But it's my yard," my wife says.

The real nuisance these days is deer. The area where we live is like a sprawling five-hundred-square-mile salad bar, with enough wooded area to give deer cover. They're everywhere, and they eat just about anything that's green and will eventually blossom. It used to be they only came out at night. Now we have all-day deer roving the neighborhoods, brazen creatures, checking out hasta beds, spoiling vegetable gardens.

Until recently they left our yard alone. Then last summer they rubbed or ate the bark off a little cherry tree and killed it. Now they're in the flowerbeds on the back of our lot. We have friends whose flowerbeds look like something out of *Better Homes and Gardens*. Did look. To the deer it's all-you-can-eat. Our friends have taken precautions. So have we. We sprinkle deer repellent around the yard. It smells like sewage for a week or so. My wife is convinced it's not enough.

Someone told her about a homemade repellent. For a couple days, she says, it will look like blood in the bushes.

Do we want that, really?

The truth is that I kind of like deer in the yard. It's not uncommon to see four or five of them mosey across the lawn at daybreak. I'll walk from window to window, stand and watch for as long as they're there. When I was a kid my parents used to load me and my brother into the car in the evening. We went out driving around the countryside looking for deer. To see a deer was to come into contact with something wild, big wild; it was untamed nature. "Well, kids," they'd say when we got home, "we saw six deer tonight. Not too bad." East of town was a farmer who kept a couple deer in a pen. It totally robbed them of their dignity and grandeur. They were like skinny, nervous cows.

My cousin had a pet deer for a short time. He got his picture in the paper. "Merritt Youth and His Pet Fawn Flag." His uncle Alfred was out in the fields on a tractor, mowing wheat, and he ran over and killed a fawn. When he stopped the rig and jumped out he found another one. He showed my cousin.

My aunt let him keep it. They fed the fawn from a baby bottle. It had sharp feet and tended to kick. It had dark, worried eyes. Of course my cousin wanted to sleep with it, and did for a few nights, until my aunt got sick of dealing with deer urine in the bed. I think they put a dog collar on it and tied it to a tree for a while. There were no deer obedience schools in the area. My cousin would let it run free, then call out to it, Flag! Flag! and it would come running home. One day when he untied it, it ran and ran and disappeared back into nature.

"WE NEED STRONGER STUFF," my wife says one night. We're lying in bed. I've checked the ceiling. I know what she's thinking. The deer could be out there right now, eating her cannas. "We should find out about that spray Jill uses."

Our friend Jill has a company come out twice a year. They spray the deer away. Supposedly it works. It's not cheap.

"It's organic," my wife says.

Over the next couple days I look at our options. On Amazon I can buy something called "The Scarecrow," a heat-and motion-activated sprinkler that emits three-second blasts of water. It sounds better than poison or blood in the bushes. But we would need a lot of them. The reviews are mixed, ranging from junk, particularly the Scarecrows made in China, to panacea. One frustrated consumer, Susan Weed (her real name), writes, "This item discourages the rabbits only when the water actually sprays them, and they soon learn where they can eat that is not in the line of the sensor." A company named Havahart markets electronic stakes. Not, as some deer haters might imagine, something to drive through the heart of a deer. You position the stakes strategically in order to deliver electric shocks to deer; small children are not exempt.

Other options include bars of soap hung from tree branches, eightpenny nails on stakes, putrescent eggs, human hair, hot sauce, and coyote urine. Chelsea, a seventh grader in Pennsylvania, for her science fair project actually conducted an empirical study of preventatives and concluded that putrid eggs and hair win the day. The commercial products she tested did not finish strong.

Google, of course, will take you down rabbit holes (and ant hills). Following a link to deer antler spray I'm taken to a site picturing a youngish stud and Jackie Stallone, Rocky's mother. They swear by a product called Nutronics, the active ingredient of which is, among other things, deer antler velvet. Something tells me this elixir will appeal primarily to yearning boy-men. The product raises testosterone levels, boosts endurance, and increases libido in both men and women. (Oh, Jackie.) A one-time purchase for a thirty-day supply is only $99.99.

While in Google I decide to check on pimple remedies. Mine is now a raging blemish. When I was in high school there were Stridex Medicated Pads and Clearasil. That was about it, though my father often growled, perhaps erroneously, that old-fashioned soap and water were all you needed. Today I see my options are X Out Face Wash-In, Proactiv Clear Zone, Proactiv Dark Spots Corrector, and MediNatura. There are lots of other products, all of which cost about the same as deer repellent.

BACK WHEN I WAS in high school, deep in the swamp of adolescence, solitary short boys and big-boned girls, kids with funny hair and crooked teeth and zits, found common cause and awkward company on Saturday nights. One night a throng of us went to the Temple Theater in Saginaw to see a movie. This was before there's-an-app-for-that, before Flixter. It was also before the prefab studio movieplex. The Temple was a one of those entertainment cathedrals that gloriously if briefly took you away from yourself. That night we thought we were going to see a horror film. We slumped into seats in the empty balcony, the lights dimmed, and a movie called *The Hellstrom Chronicle* began to play.

The subtitle might as well have been *The Bugs Shall Inherit the Earth*.

In 1971 Roger Ebert reviewed the movie, setting the stage thus: "*The Long Afternoon of Earth*, an uncommonly interesting science fiction novel by Brian W. Aldiss, tells of a time far in the future when the 'greenhouse effect' has warmed the planet into an endless rain forest. Only a handful of species have survived, and man co-exists with highly specialized plants and insects, barely managing to hold his own. And that is the way the world will end, if *The Hellstrom Chronicle* can be believed." (Those are Ebert's quotation marks around greenhouse effect.) It was a big screen documentary, and I'm sure it was the first time for all of us (not the first time we were all hopefully if fearfully anticipating). For an hour or so we squirmed in our seats, eating popcorn and M&Ms, pummeled by nature, wondering what kind of life we would ever have. We probably hadn't heard of the greenhouse effect; if we had we didn't care. I'm pretty sure we left before the movie ended.

Ebert's parting words about the film: "Think how bad the insects would feel if they could see a documentary about what humans are up to."

Whatever we're up to, it probably won't work. I have an idea that earwigs will prevail in the end. We'll be gone. The deer and mice and probably even the ants will be gone. Benevolent spiders will have gone down the tube. If not earwigs, another prehistoric-looking thing will live on and hang out in our defunct backyard for a few billion years. Oxford physicist Rafael Batista is betting on a creature called the tardigrade. It's an extremophile with eight legs, "renowned for its ability to survive where every other complex living organism cannot. The tardigrade, a micro-animal that grows up to 1.2 millimeters and can live for up to 60 years, is able to survive for 30 years without food or water, endure temperatures up to 300 F, and can even survive exposure to the vacuum of space."

But right now we've got pests. The day of my presentation we call Jill, inquiring about her approach to deer control. I discover a couple more anthills in the yard. My talk goes fine, though a few minutes before it starts a three-year-old approaches the podium, points, and asks, "What's the thing on your nose?"

A plugged-up sebaceous gland. Bacteria run amok. It will live and die, in other words *heal*, on its own.

Do what you can or leave it alone. Either way, it's got you.

# iSmell

IN THE CAR YESTERDAY I detected an unmistakable fragrance— eau de WD-40.

We have a fickle latch on the door from the garage into our house. Twice this past week I turned the key in the lock and felt the mechanism go click, then stick. Jiggle the knob all you want. There's no opening the door. I will eventually replace the knob and lock mechanism, but so far I've let myself in through another door and enjoyed trying to fix the sticky knob.

*Take it apart and put it back together.* That's my standard repair protocol. If I take something apart and can't put it back together, well, clearly the stupid thing is busted. If I can put it back together and it still doesn't work, there is a measure of success. I did no harm. But if I can actually make something work, I am the man. Or, in gender-neutral parlance, I am the person. Yesterday, standing in the mudroom, I was the person. An efficacious repair person who knows that mechanical devices often resume smooth function when treated with that mysterious substance, that fragrant oily elixir, WD-40.

I must have got some on me. A sweet scent, a personly—no, a *manly* scent—I wore with pride. Odd. I am not now, nor have I never ever been, a fragrant man.

Like most kids, watching my father shave I was mesmerized by the rite and transported by the Old Spice he slapped on his shiny cheeks and jaw. The bottle alone, with its ocean blue galleon and red curlicue font and its peg-leg cap, was exotic. Some nights, once he was done shaving, he would pat my cheeks with his Old Spicy hands, and I would walk out of the bathroom feeling like a seafaring boy.

Then came seventh grade. In second-hour gym class my locker was next to Ronnie Fritz's. After showers one day we were dressing for our next class. He started splashing stuff on his face.

"What's that?" I said.

"Cologne." He screwed the cap on the bottle and showed me. Canoe.

Cologne, I guessed, was like aftershave only different. I was still a few years from shaving. But something told me I was ready for cologne.

"Lemme see that," I said, leaning in for a whiff.

Junior high boys were smelling up and down the hallways with Hai Karate, with English Leather. Eddie Maurer wore Jade East. Ricky Burmeister and Mike Howe swore by Brut. Dave Marolf was a British Sterling man.

"Peggy Bohnoff says she loves Canoe," Ronnie Fritz said.

It did not smell like a canoe, which is probably good. It smelled like a floral disinfectant. I upended the bottle, wet an index finger, and daubed some on my jaw. Ronnie nodded encouragement. He said I would be a girl magnet. I shook a few drops into my hand, rubbed Canoe on my cheeks, then a few more drops, and then a few more, applying it generously, luxuriously, all over my face. We closed our lockers, tied our shoes, and went to class.

It was social studies with Mrs. Smith until 11:28; then lunch. I sat in the right rear corner of the room. About five minutes into class I realized I was too much in the Canoe. I tried to pay attention to what was what happening in class, but I all could do was picture the fumes rising from my upper body, shimmering in the air around me, a toxic chemical aura. I looked around. No one seemed to notice, but I was in agony. I had to do something. I couldn't wait until lunch; I was asphyxiating myself. Finally I went to Mrs. Smith's desk and asked to be excused to go the bathroom, where

I pulled down lengths of brown paper towel, wetted them in the sink, and scrubbed my face, trying to erase the scent. I pumped foamy white soap from the dispenser and sozzled it around my palms, lathering my chin, cheeks, and upper lip, then rinsed and regarded my red face in the mirror, trying to smell myself.

Back in class a few minutes passed. I lifted my hands to my face, sniffed at the air around me, feeling flammable. I reeked. I told myself: I will never do this again.

Certain days back then, when the wind came out of the northwest, you could smell Dow Chemical in my hometown. The plant was eight miles up the road in Midland. It gave off an acrid smell, a chemical stench that surprised you every time in much the way, years later, the smell of wet tobacco pervading the air in Durham, North Carolina, took me by surprise. The thing is, you couldn't *not* smell Dow on those days. Driving through Midland, past rust-colored tanks, past switching stations and distillation units connected by endless intricate networks of green pipe and valves, you could close your eyes and unsee the industrial sprawl and the sick greenish air. But there was no escaping the odor molecules pinging across your olfactory receptors.

It is commonly thought the human sense of smell is underwhelming, nowhere near as powerful and accurate as that of other creatures. Humans are sight-dominant, perhaps because we walk upright. We have noses, not snouts. D. C. McCullough, writing for the *Guardian*, takes the contrary position, observing that our sense of smell is both instantaneous and "highly specific, and accurate, not unlike the spectroscope, a scientific instrument that can faultlessly identify atoms inside and the molecules they make up by measuring molecular vibrations." Odd, if true, because the language we use to describe scent is nothing if not minimal, even impoverished. Smells good. Smells bad. Smells sweet, sour, floral, rotten . . . Yet smell scientists celebrate the human nose. According to *PLOS Biology*, "Humans outperform the most sensitive measuring instruments such as the gas chromatograph. These results indicate that humans are not poor smellers (a condition technically called microsmats), but rather are relatively good, perhaps even excellent, smellers (macrosmats)."

There are definitely super smellers, those in the perfume industry, for example, and those in the food and wine industry. Wine tasting, most oenologists will tell you, is 85 percent nose. Their olfactory appraisal involves both the orthonasal route (the, as it were, *schnase*) and the retronasal route (the olfactory apparatus in the back of the oral cavity). One of my winehead friends tells me that after you taste a wine you can't scent it full-on again in that sitting. "Do all your nose work first," he says. (If he is right, this is the second reason I would never want to taste WD-40.)

In *Somm*, the 2012 movie about four sommeliers preparing to take master exams, an individual lowers his nose to a glass of white wine, inhales, and delivers this bouquet profile: "On the nose this wine is clean, no obvious flaws. This wine has a moderate-plus intensity. This wine is youthful. It's showing bruised aromas: bruised apple, bruised pear, bruised peach, honeysuckle, chamomile, lavender, slight botrytis, limestone, wet wool, hay, pistachio, tea." All that? Really? Lavender and wet wool in the same glass? While I'm skeptical and impatient with winespeak, I am also willing to defer to a good nose. My wife will identify an ingredient in a complex dish immediately. She'll smell and taste, turn to me, and say confidently and usually correctly, *It's tarragon, obviously*. One evening a friend, invited to our house for dinner, brought her prized dessert and invited us to guess her secret ingredient. She stumped my wife and me. Then our son smelled it and tasted. "Pear," he said without a moment's hesitation. Adding, "I hate pear."

I don't know if I'm microsmat or macrosmat as much as, in given situations, like my son, antismat.

In high school and college I briefly flirted again with fragrance. This time it was musk. Men wore it, women wore it—the scent seemed elemental, earthy, and powerful. Maybe, I thought, if I could grow a mustache, I could wear musk and not feel like a complete fool. But the more I smelled it the more it struck me as too powerful, so overwhelming I would be back in the canoe, totally conspicuously smelly.

For years in the classroom I was subjected to a dizzying range of scents as I stood at the podium while fragrant students filed in, both men and women, redolent with manufactured odors—shampoos and conditioners, colognes and perfumes, lotions and body washes, deodorants—aggressive smells often applied in profusion, frequently to the point of bringing tears to my eyes. You could classify student scents: candy shop, flower shop, candle store, compost pile, with an occasional blast of ashtray. Smell posed a real occupational challenge. If you had asked me, I would have said smell chemistry, as it pertains to the production of smells we sell and buy, has been a dismal fail.

And yet progress marches on. Coming soon to a cell phone near you: digital smell. How long before we can access every imaginable fragrance on iSmell? What a world. *Dude, smell this: it's bacon!*

Scientists have zeroed in on smell at the center of our galaxy. They're out there looking for amino acids and the origin of life, and in a dust cloud they find ethyl formate, the chemical smell of raspberries. Closer to home astronauts in orbit say food has little or no smell or taste in the zero-gravity zone. Space, their noses tell them, when they bring the scent of it in on their space suits, smells like burnt steak, hot metal, or welding fumes.

Imagine life without smell. If I were up there feeling earthsick I might want to open Google Scent and click on freshly cut grass or burning leaves or pumpkin pie. Or maybe Old Spice.

# 17

# Alarm

MY CELLPHONE RINGS AT 6:30 on a Saturday morning.

"Who could that be?" my wife says. She's drinking coffee and reading at the kitchen table. She's deep into a book about the French Revolution, written in Italian by some guys who call themselves Wu Ming. Sometimes she kind of disappears on me. I have to call her back. I'm trying to tell her about a song I heard at the gym the other day while I was on the treadmill.

"It was old Pink Floyd," I say.

"Hmmm."

"'Be Careful with That Ax, Eugene'?"

She nods a nod that could say anything: *No, I don't remember Pink Floyd.* Or: *This sentence I'm reading is written in the subjunctive.* Or: *I married a fool.*

"Isn't that funny?" I start to say, *You know, the ax, and you're reading about the French Revolution?*

She shakes her head, doesn't look up. "And I'm supposed to know that song?"

"It took me back to high school days."

"Aren't you going to answer that?"

I'm letting the phone ring. An 877 area code shows on the display. It's nobody we know, I say.

As soon as that call goes dead our landline phone rings. Now we look at each other. Something is up. Feeling a mixture of curiosity and dread, I answer after the third ring.

The voice on the other end is garbled. All I understand is, am I Richard Bailey?

"What?" I say.

More garble. It's a female voice.

"Who is this?" I ask.

Third time, I understand: it's a security service. The alarm on our daughter's house has been activated, we're on the call list, am I Richard Bailey, would I go over there, walk around the house and check things out. And do I have the security code so I can I reset the alarm?

I tell her I don't have the code. "Is it making noise?" I ask.

The security service doesn't know if the alarm makes noise. They can't shut it off and they can't reset it. They can't do anything. She says she's calling from Washington.

"D C ?"

"No, the other one," she says. All she knows is the alarm went off. Do I have the code?

"No," I say, "I don't know the code." But I guess I could drive over and have a look.

"Will you please call us," she says, "when you find out what's going on?"

It's the noise that worries me. Once a month the alarmed house behind us breaks into a horn-and-siren song, usually around this time of day. For a few seconds it's kind of funny. I imagine surprise, confusion, and panic back there, the startled dentist or her husband lurching to silence the alarm. They are right to lurch. If the sound went longer than it does, it would not be funny to anyone nearby. My daughter's house—she and her husband have lived there a few months—is fifteen minutes away by car. They're out of town for the holiday. I don't know what their alarm sounds like. It could be terrible. It could be blasting right now.

On the road I call my daughter a few times to ask about the code. She's in Seattle, where it's currently four o'clock in the morning. It could be hours before I can reach her. I drive a little over the speed limit and give myself permission to cautiously run a few red lights. I figure if I get pulled over I'll invite the cop to come with me. On radio news they're talking about the two-year-old in Walmart who shot and killed his mother with her gun; an unhappy son in Florida has decapitated his mother. Customs officers on the U.S. side of the Ambassador Bridge had to shoot a guy. He was on foot brandishing a gun, which turned out to be a toy. The news story said they shot him in the arm, which, you know, must be an accident. There's all that and ordinary mayhem. And I'm driving to a potential break-in armed with a cellphone.

Some of my friend have guns. In my situation I suppose they would pack heat.

I KEEP A RIFLE next to my bed at home. I went through a phase.

It's a Daisy BB gun, a blue one. To fend off assaults of wanton squirrels I kept the gun loaded and ready. Whenever I saw them gorging themselves on the bird feeder that hangs from an apple tree in our yard, I climbed the stairs to my perch, cocked the weapon, and slid the window open, careful to keep the BBs from rolling audibly inside the gun. It wasn't quite shooting fish in a barrel; neither was it a feat of marksmanship. I'd get the squirrel in the sights, aim for its hindquarters, and squeeze off a shot. There would be a coughlike report from the weapon, a projectile I could actually see speeding in the direction of my prey, and *ping!* the squirrel would be airborne, launching itself from the feeder and running to safety. Once it was out of range it would usually stop and scratch itself.

I was protecting my bird feeder. It was satisfying. And kind of thrilling.

"You hurt them," my wife said one day.

"Not much," I said.

"How do you know?" she asked. "How do you know you don't kill them?"

It's a nonlethal force, I said.

She shook her head. I could guess what was going through her mind: *I didn't think I married a killer.*

"A pellet gun would kill them," I said. "But a BB gun just goes *ping!*" I made a fun face; it had no effect on her. "It just teaches them a lesson," I added. What I couldn't say was, it's *fun*. And, to be honest, it didn't teach them a lesson. The squirrels kept coming back. They were hungry. It was free food.

One day, driving home from work, I saw a squirrel lying by the side of the road. It didn't look flattened or smashed. It was not taking a nap. I suppose its little tongue was sticking out. I wondered: Did I do that?

So now the gun sits there, next to the window, a reminder of my bent chromosome. The bird feeder is baffled. I solved that problem. The squirrels don't even try. I notice the gun some nights when I get ready for bed and imagine hearing an intruder downstairs. One of my friends said once that the most terrifying words a burglar can hear as he tiptoes around your house are: "I have a shotgun." How about "I have an ax"?

I have a BB gun.

ON THE TURN INTO my daughter's neighborhood I put my window down, relieved to hear silence. At the next corner I look for squad car flashers. Nothing. Is that good? I pull into the driveway, shut the engine off, and sit. The house looks normal. To feel a little less alone I call the security company back. I get a different helper, give the address. Any minute I'm expecting sirens and horns. The alarm probably goes on and off until it's reset.

"Is the alarm still on?" I ask.

He says it is.

"I don't hear anything," I say.

"It's on," he says. Did I walk around the house?

"Not yet, "I say. "I guess I could."

"Do you have the code?"

"I told you I don't have the code," I say. "Write that down."

I get out of the car, climb to the front porch, test the doorknob, giving the door a push and pull, half expecting the alarm to start blaring. The door is locked. The latch gives off a tiny metallic click when I pull it shut. That might mean something. I step off the porch and decide to go clockwise around the house: side windows and living room windows (good), two sliding glass doors in the back (good). When I get around to the side door into the garage I execute my push/pull and the door swings open. I step back. There's enough light to see the door casing is intact. No forcible entry. At least at this door. I try the handle—the door is unlocked—then lean forward and peer into the dark garage. How far do I go with this? I recall my father's advice in these matters: Don't go in there.

Years ago, living in the city, whenever I pulled in the driveway I always thought to myself, *Today might be the day.* The day we're burgled. One day the front door was open. The cops came in a blue squad car. "Tactical Unit" was written on this side. While my daughter and I stood at the edge of the road next to the big maple they went in the house, stepping back out after a few minutes, pronouncing the house secure. Another day we unlocked the back door, went inside, and my daughter ran through the kitchen and into the living room, where she began to scream hysterically. *This is the day,* I thought. It turned out a grackle with a bad sense of direction had flown down the chimney and into the house. I subdued it with a tennis racket. Gently.

No, I decide. I'm not going any further.

I go back to the car, pull out my phone, and call the cops.

It's ten or fifteen minutes before a patrol car stops at the edge of the drive. It's one of those black s u vs. It looks menacing in the dark. "Evidence Unit" is written on the side. The lone cop is hatless, tall and thin, twenty-five or thirty years younger than I am. He tells me one in ten thousand times it's a real break-in. I report what I've found, noticing as I do that his clothes don't fit him very well. The pants are too baggy on him. The waist-length jacket he's wearing hangs crooked on his frame. The whole outfit looks borrowed. On a cold morning like this I'd think a longer, warmer jacket would be in order. When he turns toward the house I see his gun, exposed and ready on his hip.

A few minutes later he's back.

"The side door was open," he tells me.

I thought I said that.

"Otherwise, everything seems okay."

I tell him I'm worried about the alarm going off again and disturbing the neighbors.

"The alarm company," I tell him, "says the alarm is still on."

"Usually it makes noise *inside* the house," he says, "to spook the bad guys." He reaches down, takes hold of his jacket with both hands, tries to straighten it. It still looks crooked. "You got a key to the house?" he says. "You can reset the alarm if you want to. Do you have the code?"

WHEN I GET HOME my wife is sitting on the couch reading her Wu Ming.

"All clear?" she says.

There's no break-in, I say. "But the alarm is still on. At the home office, out in Washington, they're on high alert."

"A lot of good that does." She turns a page. "But no noise, right? It's not disturbing the neighbors?"

"The cop says the noise is inside the house."

That settles it. She nods and returns to her reading. I tell her Wu Ming sounds like the name of a group, a string quartet.

I wonder what sound an alarm would make inside a house. Maybe they give you choices: sirens, bells, buzzers, horns; beeping, screeching, wailing; outer space noise, static. You tailor the alarm to your lifestyle. I look out the window at the bird feeder. A nuthatch is scraping seed off the feeder onto the ground. The squirrels are gorging themselves. If I were to install an alarm I'd ask for the blood-curdling screams in "Be Careful with That Ax, Eugene."

I'm sure it could be arranged.

# 18

# Up a Creak

WE NOTICED IT HER second or third year of college.

When our daughter called home it was definitely there, audible in phone calls. You worry about your kids, how college will change them. We passed the phone back and forth, heard all the updates—classes, friends, work, money. Then, after closing the call, we sat and looked at each other. Nothing prepared us for what was happening.

My wife said, "Did you hear it?"

I told her yes, I heard something.

"What's going on?"

I couldn't tell. This was, like, 2006? I wanted to reassure my wife, to say it was nothing, but I heard it, too. Sometimes it was obvious; other times it was clearly our daughter's old voice. Clearly *her*. But in the end we knew this new thing was really there. At the ends of sentences her voice trailed away, falling into a lower register, and then, just before silence and the taking of breath, there was a faint, prolonged scratchiness as the last syllable died away.

It was vocal fry, also known as creak.

The *Dictionary of Linguistics and Phonetics* describes it "as a very slow vibration of only one end of the vocal folds." The more popular definition: "a glottal, creaking sound of lower-register speech oscillation." Conventional wisdom is that creak is usually heard in the speech of young women, and it's a very BIG DEAL. Or it's not. It is described as both heartbreaking and harmless.

I was surprised recently to discover that I've caught the creak.

I heard it a few nights ago. We were in the car, on our way to the Imperial Bar, a taco joint in Ferndale. In town from New York, my son and his girlfriend sat in the back seat of the car chatting, both of them clearly creaking out at the ends of their sentences.

"They've got great hot dogs at Imperial," my son said. "You gonna have one, Mom?"

She said no, she didn't think so.

"Dad?"

"Yeah," I said. Only it sounded like *yeaaaaahh,* like the end of the word was being pressed through a cheese grater.

When did that start? I wondered. Do I creak because my kids do? They've been out of the house for years. What's going on?

Viruses sweep through our language, infecting us. Well, some of us. Suddenly, for example, an expression like "go figure" pops up in everyone's speech. These days people are actually saying BFF and LOL out loud. And the word "like"? We're well into a like epidemic. It's, like, expressive in a useful way. Like has also morphed into a verb of speech. (I'm like, Seriously, where did you get those shoes? And she's, like, You'll never even guess.) Like is handy and annoying, and apparently it's here to stay. Some people love like; many hate it. Few people are like-neutral.

Creak is also described as an epidemic. But it's different. It's not new lingo that will arrive, thrive, and eventually, we hope, fade into cliché. (Witness "think outside the box," on the same page with "at the end of the day," trending downward; seriously, I hope they are.) Creak is a gradual and pervasive shift in intonation, and, like "like," it appears to be here to stay.

These things happen.

In the early eighties, as a graduate student, I was in a poetry workshop at the University of Michigan. Once a week we each brought a poem we had written to class, distributed copies, read our work out loud, and heard it talked about by ten or twelve classmates. Every session, at one end of the conference table, there sat two young women in the MFA program. They were both from East

Coast liberal arts colleges. They would say things like, "I'm not sure about the end of this poem? I think it's unearned?" "Some of these line breaks bother me?" "There might be sexism, you know? in the poem's reference to brown-skinned women?" It was my first encounter with uptalk.

Next thing I knew, I mean over the next few years, everyone was uptalking. Kids, both female and male, became addicted to the high rising terminal (HRT). Where our kids went to school, sentences often began with an HRT "actually." As in: "Actually? I had pizza for dinner last night?" "Actually? I'm pretty good at math?" At the dinner table, when my wife and I heard our kids uptalking we got right in their faces, so much that I know they started to hate us. "You're uptalking," we'd say when they were in midsentence at the kitchen table. They rolled their eyes. They repeated what they said in level-talk. Those interruptions were cruel and unusual. An attack on a person's speech, particularly if it occurs when the person is in midsentence, is rude, harsh, and deeply personal. It can be borderline abuse. But it seemed necessary to us. The linguistic equivalent of tough love.

One night I was telling my wife about something that happened at work. It was a good story. It mattered to me. Just as I was getting to the good part she stopped me in midsentence. "You're uptalking," she said.

I thought for a minute, playing back what I'd just said.

"Maybe just a little, but . . ."

"More than a little."

"Okay, but . . ."

"I just thought you would want to know."

"I do want to know," I said. Whereas, really, I didn't. Or I did. Just not then. I was trying to say something.

The trouble is that uptalk and creak can change the way we listen. They can interfere with how *well* we listen.

Kai Ryssdal, on his Marketplace broadcast, recently interviewed a couple in Los Angeles, Rose and Warren Schwartz, who just opened a soft-serve ice cream shop. I like ice cream. I like stories about plucky startups. This was a good story. What was striking throughout, though, was Rose's creak. (She creaked; Warren did not.) I couldn't wait for Rose to talk. Will she do it? I couldn't wait for the tail end of her sentences, when her intonation dropped and her voice got scratchy and then went to pieces. As I listened I became keenly aware of the fact that I wasn't *really listening* to what Rose was saying. Only to how she said it.

Naomi Wolf, writing for the *Guardian*, says that creak is heart-breaking. "It is *because* these young women are so empowered," she observes, "that our culture assigned them a socially appropriate mannerism that is certain to tangle their steps and trivialise their important messages to the world." Hold on. I have trouble with the "our culture assigned them" claim here, because it oversimplifies what we do with language and how we happen to do it, and how it shapes us. In addition, my ear tells me it's not just women who are creaking and frying. Men do it too. I do it, my son does it. The other day I listened to Fareed Zakaria interview J. D. Vance, author of *Hillbilly Elegy*. Born in Ohio, raised in West Virginia, reared in a language community where creak is a body of water, not a linguistic oddity, Vance is now a Yale-educated lawyer. He makes his living in finance when he's not joining Sunday morning "powerhouse roundtables" that explain the week's news to audiences across the country. In the ten-minute interview Vance couldn't finish a sentence without creaking. Was he "assigned" the mannerism? Or did he just start talking that way because he occupies a certain linguistic universe?

Men, it is true, can creak with impunity. In men a dropping register and glottal croaking is authoritative. See/hear Noam Chomsky. In a study conducted at the University of California, Berkeley, seven young men and seven young women were recorded saying, "Thank you for considering me for this opportunity" in normal voice and in creaky voice. Next, four hundred male and four hundred female listeners reacted to the recorded voices. All the listeners preferred normal voice. Most of them found female creak more problematic, ranking those women "less trustworthy" than males with creaky voices.

"Young, urban women are the leaders of language change," says Auburn Barron-Lutzross, a linguist at Berkeley. "So when something new happens [in female speech], people will become critical and maybe even disturbed and say, 'That's not how the language is supposed to sound!' But it will continue to spread."

Spoken English, grouches say, should not sound like that.

Who's most annoyed? Ira Glass says, "If people are having a problem with [creak and vocal fry], what it means is they're old." Often it also means they are male.

WE ORDER HOT DOGS at the Imperial, all of us but my wife, who is a purist and will only eat a grilled (not boiled) ballpark dog. It's her loss. These are bacon-wrapped Sonoran dogs, "haute dogs," a new trend getting traction in the U.S., an import from Mexico. They are spicy, complex flavor bombs that are radically reorienting wiener cuisine across the country.

It's a warm summer night. The roll-up doors fronting Woodward Avenue are flung open. People are lined up outside waiting to get in. Our server, a thin young guy with his hair tied up in a man bun, swoops in and takes our order. Behind him, young urbans and families lean toward each other, eating, drinking, talking. I can't tell if our server creaks. It's too noisy. But it's nice to think of mothers and their adolescent daughters, and dads and their adolescent boys, and the swarms of little kids stuffing tacos and dogs in their mouths, creaking and frying and producing a combined glottal rattle and roar.

"Good, Dad?" my son says. We tap dogs, making a nonverbal toast.

"*Yeaaaaaah*," I say. Good.

# 19

# At Least It's Not Terrible

LATELY I'VE BEEN TRYING to figure out my muddled thinking about breakfast. I suffered an epiphany of sorts this summer. We were in the Leelanau Peninsula, staying in an Airbnb place right on the lake. It should have been heavenly. The scenery *was* heavenly. The house, on the other hand, was filthy. It might have been cleaned. The bedding looked refreshed. The towels were washed, folded, put away. The white walls and empty glass shelves inside the fridge were practically blinding. But what empty fridge doesn't shock you into thinking it's clean?

The problem was very specific. Ratty furniture that my wife was reluctant to sit on, including a squash-colored chair my son-in-law thought smelled faintly of urine. And flies. There were dead flies everywhere. This was a long ranch with sliding glass doors on either end of the house, facing the water. At the base of the doors, as though they had killed themselves trying to escape by flinging themselves hopelessly against the glass, were the carcasses of flies. Hundreds of them, I would say.

"We have to shop," my wife said.

"I'll sweep," I said.

"No, we have to shop, now, for cleaning supplies. Have you seen the shower?"

I didn't need to see it. What I needed to do was get my wife to the IGA as fast as possible. Over the next few hours she would bleach areas of the house that were in critical condition, and I would busy myself with overt acts of sympathetic cleaning. We would get through the next few days. But for her the weekend vacation was already, and would continue to be until we closed the door behind us on Sunday, a bust.

Breakfast, I remember thinking. Tomorrow we'll have a nice breakfast.

Breakfast can fix almost anything.

Or maybe not. I've begun to think that breakfast is overrated, possibly the most hazardous meal of the day.

HERE IN ITALY, WHERE we are staying for six weeks or so, I'm happy to start the day with an Italian breakfast—coffee and a pastry. So is my wife. Once or twice a week, a few hours after we get out of bed, after we've already had a few cups of coffee, I'll have a brioche with chocolate or pastry cream inside. She usually has a *girella*, which is a flat coiled pastry with raisins.

"I would never eat this at home," I say to her one morning.

At home in the States I have yogurt with nuts and honey. I make a fruit and vegetable smoothie. Eat a pastry? Never.

We're in a coffee bar next to the gas station down the road from our apartment. Standing at the bar, stirring sugar into their espressos, are half a dozen very thin people, all of them enjoying their pastry breakfast. This morning I'm having brioche with some kind of jam in it.

My wife takes a bite from hers, not her usual *girella*.

"And you?" I say. "Would you eat a donut for breakfast at home?"

"This is a pastry," she says, avoiding the question, "not a donut."

"That," I tell her, pointing at the thing she is eating, "is a donut."

It's a *bombolone* (note the first four letters of the word), which is either a tube or bun of fried dough that is filled with pastry cream and rolled in sugar. She ate them when she was a kid. It's a nostalgia food. Ordinarily she shows restraint. Standing at the coffee bar after we order cappuccino, she asks about (not for) bombolone, then gazes longingly at them behind panes of glass in the pastry case. Briefly she turns toward me with a look of profound sadness; I see her resolve weakening. Usually, however, she stays strong and sticks with the *girella*.

We eat these things because they are there and we are here. I don't always feel good about it. They do not engender feelings of virtue.

THE NEXT MORNING IN Leelanau, sitting in the urinous chair, I suggest we go out for breakfast. I'm thinking up-north breakfast, something ample, lumberjacky. My wife plans to attack the kitchen today. She will find crumbs, more flies, and generalized dirt. I figure we'll need a good compensatory breakfast before the cleaning begins.

"It would be nice to find a place that has nice fresh vegetables," she says.

We walk into town and try a mom-and-pop place. It has a boardwalk out front. Inside it has up-north rustic appeal: maps of the lake decoupaged on table tops, stuffed fish and nautical junk mounted on the knotty pine walls, gingham curtains.

On the menu eggs, fatty meats, and carbs.

No heart smart. Strictly heart dumb.

On the menu we find French toast, pancakes and waffles, muffins and pastries, fried potatoes in various iterations, artery-clogging breakfast meats like bacon, link and patty sausage, fried ham, to say nothing of eggs fried in soybean oil, no doubt with antifoaming additives. What makes these items taste good is the crap you squeeze, squirt, and spread over them. I mean maple syrup (sweetened with high-fructose corn syrup), assorted fruit jams and jellies (sweetened with high-fructose corn syrup), ketchup (sweetened with high-fructose corn syrup), and artificial butter.

My wife orders the vegetable skillet. I order ham and eggs and potatoes with dry toast. I'm sure the pale green vegetables in her skillet were fresh at one time, and I'm sure somewhere in the restaurant supply business there is a better confection to brighten a piece of industrialized whole wheat toast this morning than mixed fruit jelly.

We eat, we are filled, we are mildly disappointed.

We are filled.

There's a what-the-hell-ness in our attitude about breakfast out. We'll eat breakfast in a restaurant where we wouldn't think of ordering lunch or dinner. When we vet restaurants for evenings out our criterion is often *I want something I can't get at home.* You know what you want—perfectly cooked sashimi tuna; a paper-thin, tender beef carpaccio. At breakfast forget vetting. We eat stuff and think, *I would never want this at home.* We tend to take what we can get. There's a place by the side of the road. That'll do. Perfunctory eggs, gummy pancakes, ersatz ham; for your toast, mixed fruit. It's not great, but hey, we're on vacation.

"It was all right," my wife says afterward.

"No it wasn't," I say.

"At least it wasn't terrible," she says.

BACK AT THE HOUSE there's cleaning to be done. We get through it. She gets through it and later joins us down by the water, where we swat flies that would like to come inside the house and die.

Sunday morning, on the way home, we stop for breakfast at a place in Traverse City called Frenchies. They have a breakfast enchilada with braised pork and green sauce. It doesn't look anything like breakfast. I can't get something like it at home. It's way, way better than not terrible.

WE READ OF "THE FRENCH paradox." The French eat bread, cheeses, and foods cooked in butter and anointed with buttery sauces, they enjoy fattening desserts, yet they are not fat. It may not be in our lingo, but there is an Italian paradox as well. How do they eat pastries every morning and stay thin? While we're here my wife and I eat them too, feeling every bit like sinners, which probably makes them taste even better.

We will get back to Detroit a few weeks before Christmas. We'll be busy. There will be shopping to do. One morning we may find ourselves in a part of town we don't know and decide to take a chance on breakfast. I'll try to remember to pick up a jam caddy on a table, looking for mixed fruit. It's an indicator. I'll suggest to my wife that instead of this place we might as well go somewhere and eat something really terrible. Like a donut.

# 20

# Wreckage

I WAS TEN YEARS old the first time I saw a real car accident and its aftermath. It was a humid summer evening. My father and I were closing our service station when the township siren sounded. A cop car screamed through town. Then the phone rang. My father took the call, listened a few seconds, nodded, and hung up. He pointed me toward the door and said, *We have to go*.

Half a mile out of town a fire truck was already on the scene, along with the cop car, their headlights trained on a station wagon flipped on its top in the middle of an intersection. Another car was nose-down in a ditch, its engine still running, tail lights on, a turn signal flashing. I stayed in the car while my father got out and talked to the constable. Sitting on the pavement next to the overturned car was a large man, naked to the waist and barefoot. His legs were crossed in front of him. He was bleeding from the head; more blood was visible on his chest and stomach. Every so often he lowered a hand to the ground to steady himself. I learned later that the driver of the other car was a local man the constable and firemen knew, that they joked with him as they pulled him from his car.

We rushed back to town for our wrecker and then returned to the accident, where we righted the overturned car and winched the other car out of the ditch. At some point my father handed me a shop broom. I swept up broken glass, listening to the crackle and tinny voices coming from the cop car radio, avoiding the spot on the road where the bleeding man had been made to lie down.

Eventually, in the distance, there was another siren as an ambulance bore down on us and came to take the injured men away.

We towed both cars into town, leaving them at one of the car dealers. In the cab of the wrecker my father patted my leg and asked if I was all right.

"You saw something tonight," he said.

"I'm okay."

"Are you sure?" He patted my leg again and said he thought if I had trouble sleeping that night I might stay home from school and sleep late the next day.

I think of this experience, even to this day, whenever I see car parts at the side the road, on the shoulder, in the median, at the edge of a ditch. It's a common sight these days. You see the shiny decorative crosshatching of a grill, fender liners, smooth black plastic splash guards, whole bumpers, sometimes an entire front-end module. It's a new kind of litter, all this lightweight wreckage left behind (I don't recall ever seeing a heavy, shiny chrome bumper along the road when I was a kid). Even more striking is the sight of a smashed car on a truck bed that passes you on the road. Suddenly the perfunctory mortal danger of your commute to work or your trip to the grocery store or to Home Depot becomes apparent. There's death out there. In *Lives of the Cell* Lewis Thomas speaks of "death in the open," how unnatural it is to see an animal's remains along the road. "It is always a queer shock," he writes, "part a sudden upwelling of grief, part unaccountable amazement. . . . The outrage is more than just the location; it is the impropriety of such visible death, anywhere."

Must we be reminded?

On the other hand, what if we want to be reminded?

This woman named Lenore worked out at the facility where my wife and I go. She was tall and thin, well into her seventies I would say. She kept her brown hair cut in a bob and had about her a natural elegance and athleticism. Three days a week we would see her reading while walking the treadmill, working muscle groups on the machines with her eyes closed in concentration.

I asked her one day, "Were you a dancer?"

She blushed. "Why do you ask?"

"It's your hands," I said, "the way you hold them when you bend."

She said yes, she had studied dance, a long time ago.

I was afraid I had embarrassed her and tried not to watch her on our days after that, but there was something so poised and collected and unself-conscious about her movement: I wanted to look.

Then she missed a few days. She told my wife she wasn't sleeping well. Then she missed a few more days. And then she stopped coming altogether. She died in just a few months, without having visitors, without returning telephone calls.

Thomas takes the long view, noting that all the billions of us on earth today are on "the same schedule.... All of that immense mass of flesh and bone and consciousness will disappear by absorption into the earth, without recognition by the transient survivors." I know this and accept it. What are the options? Nevertheless, every so often I find myself standing by the side of the road, a transient survivor, shocked and diminished, grasping for hands that are not there.

# 21

# About Your Stuff

SHE SAYS I SHOULD have kept the anvil.

It was a real blacksmith's anvil that belonged to my dad, before him to my grandfather, before him I don't know who. This was no beginner's anvil. Coal black, it had felt the heat of a forge and the beat of hammers for a hundred years or more. It had a bick, or a horn, for hammering curved pieces of metal, it had a step and a pritchel hole, it had a smooth face with a rounded edge on one side. It sat on a log end. Anvil and log together I'm guessing weighed somewhere in the area of two hundred fifty pounds.

Both my father and grandfather had shops.

My wife and I have a back porch.

The anvil, she says, would have looked nice on the back porch. I don't disagree. I could picture it out there on a summer evening, next to the potted ferns, a glass of white wine sitting on it. But I just said no. I could also picture myself having to lift it, first getting it into the car, arguably the wrong vehicle for transporting an anvil, then to our house from my parents' house, then from the car to the back porch, then to various locations on the porch, finding just the right spot.

A while back I saw a cartoon in *The New Yorker*. A father and son are standing in front of a garage. The big door is open. Inside, on every square inch of available space from floor to ceiling, is a jumble of stuff. The father is saying: "One day all of this will be yours."

The story of late middle age might be written as follows: You lose your parents, you gain their stuff.

The spring our parents died, within a few months of each other, my brother and I came into this difficult inheritance. It was all ours. We flirted with the idea of various kinds of sales—a garage sale, a rummage sale, an estate sale. We couldn't decide which. We knew we had to get rid of stuff. We also knew that most of our parents' stuff wasn't worth much, and that the measures we were considering would be insufficient. Some of their stuff, probably a lot of it, would still be there, all of it ours, to dispose of.

Four consecutive Fridays I drove ninety miles north to the house. My brother and I walked around the basement, out to the garage and Dad's shop, into the bedrooms still full of their clothes and shoes. We opened and closed kitchen cabinets and drawers. We filled garbage bags with magazines and empty plastic margarine containers and took them to the road. On a shelf above a coat closet our dad had twenty-six bill caps. One day we found in a living room drawer greeting cards my mother had saved, Happy Father's Day cards, Happy Anniversary cards, Happy Birthday cards, each with two or three lines she had written. "I am so glad you are my husband." "I love you more with each passing year." "I never imagined I could love someone so much."

Each day, after a morning of these half-hearted exertions, freighted with love and futility, we sank into living room chairs and talked in our own little theater of memory.

A decision was required.

Do not resuscitate. It felt like that.

I'VE BEEN HEARING DOWNSIZING stories lately. Few of us are the right size. Some people my age talk of going small.

I know a woman who sold everything and moved to Italy, with all her belongings in two suitcases. Now she's moving back, still with two suitcases. A couple in Michigan retired, sold everything, and moved to Colorado. Another couple in Michigan retired, sold everything, and moved to Los Angeles. A friend of mine on Facebook confessed recently, "We have 49 beach towels. How did that happen? Who the hell needs 49 beach towels?"

Reading up on downsizing leads me to an organization called the Simplicity Collective, a name rich in paradox. They are apostles of Thoreau. On their website there is pulldown menu dedicated to Thoreau: Thoreau on clothing, Thoreau on shelter, Thoreau on food. Thoreau on comforts, luxuries, and tools. Below the Simplicity Collective in my Google search is the Simplicity Institute. It envisions "voluntary simplicity," "a prosperous descent."

I get it. A few months each year my wife and I leave hearth and home in Detroit (part hearth and home, part museum, archive, and warehouse). We leave and go to stay in the family apartment in my wife's village in the Republic of San Marino. In the weeks before we leave we get the house ready. While we're gone the mail will have to be stopped, the grass cut, and water to toilets, the water heater, and the washing machine shut off. The last few days I try to limit recreational grocery shopping. The first time we went for a long stay, the first time I cleared out the fridge, just the jars (jams, preserves, olives, condiments) and dried up rinds of cheeses and fugitive bread crusts hiding in the back of shelves filled a garbage bag. Now it's a deliberate campaign: eat everything in the refrigerator and the freezer. The day before departure, all that's left is a carton of milk, a couple slices of bread, and two eggs.

Each time I open that almost-empty refrigerator to this amazing flash of light on the bright glass shelves and white walls, it's a revelation of possibility. We too could be minimal. Just this much, you think, and no more.

Our living space in San Marino is around a thousand square feet. We don't use all of it. In the kitchen cupboard are five glasses, six coffee cups. Above the sink in a strainer are six plates and four soup bowls. The refrigerator is a third the size of the one we have in the States. It is sufficient. We shop every day, eat most of what we buy. There's no lawn to mow, no leaves to rake. The phone rings two or three times a week. There is no mail.

Simple. And yet—

My mother-in-law's fine china, left behind when the family immigrated, fills a cabinet in the little dining room. In another cabinet, in the "great room," I count twenty-seven stem glasses, seventeen water goblets, twenty cordials. It was her good stuff, my wife says. Rattling around in a kitchen drawer are vintage accessories: ten wooden spoons, three white plastic utensils (spoon, spatula, spaghetti rake), five aluminum utensils (two ladles, a skimmer, a serving fork, an oversized spoon), two corkscrews, two can openers. And more.

In a bedroom *armadio*, taking up the space of one large cardboard box, is a pile of books, *quaderni* (notebooks), photographs, family documents. One day my wife pulls out a quaderno, reads a short essay she wrote in school when she was eight years old.

When they left San Marino for America in 1959 my wife's maternal grandmother said to my mother-in-law, "You will lose." Meaning all your stuff—the shared history, the family, your *life*—will be ripped away from you.

In that cabinet, in an *earlier* quaderno, my wife's calligraphy practice. *V v v v v v v v i i i i i i a a a a a a.*

IN THE END MY brother and I decided on an auction. A guy named Marty came to the house. We walked around the basement, out to the garage and Dad's shop, into the bedrooms.

"Goodwill should take that," Marty said, pointing at clothes hanging in their bedroom closet.

"Sure," I said. "And?"

"I can do this auction," he said. He had a team. They would come into the house for three days ahead of the sale and prepare.

I said, "What about, you know, everything that's left over?"

"We sell everything," he said.

"I don't know," my brother said. "There's probably stuff no one will want to buy."

"We sell everything," Marty said.

The day of the sale I drove north ninety miles to the house. It was a sunny day in late June. On the lawn, in the front and back and sides of the house, everything. All the furniture. On the beds of farm wagons, in boxes, everything. On tables between the farm wagons, more stuff: from half-full boxes of laundry detergent, a couple boxes of garbage bags, and plastic bags of plastic flatware already open, to two-ounce metal boxes of cinnamon, cloves, and black pepper, baking sheets and nutcrackers and mixing bowls, bug repellents, tubes of pencil leads for Dad's Eversharp pencils. Everything.

At three o'clock the cars and trucks began to arrive, parking up and down the street, many of them with trailers hitched to the vehicles. These, I later gathered, were Marty's groupies. They followed him from sale to sale. They parked and roamed, covered the territory, moving across the lawn, inspecting goods, sniffing out deals. Waiting.

The auction began at five o'clock.

Bidding on our father's chair started at $125. It sold for $35.

Bidding on the old green davenport, ugly, and with a definite slope to the center, but kept good as new, started at $100. It sold for $25.

The billcaps went for a buck.

Tom and I circulated, watched, nervous and elated. In a state of shock.

By nine o'clock, laden with our parents' stuff, vehicles crawled out of the subdivision and disappeared down the road into the dusk.

At ten o'clock house and garage and shop and yard, all were empty. Marty had sold everything. Even the garbage cans were gone.

It was a robbery, an evisceration.

It was an erasure.

Since then I've thought of these lines from *The Grapes of Wrath*, Tom Joad saying, "How can we live without our lives? How will we know it's us without our past? How will it be not to know what land's outside the door? How, if you wake up in the middle of the night and know—and *know* the willow tree's not there? Can you live without the willow tree? Well, no, you can't. The willow tree is you."

BEFORE THE AUCTION I grabbed a few tools I wanted. In particular I looked for screwdrivers, the old ones with wood handles, with dirt and sweat massaged into the grain from long years of use. They were his. Now they're mine.

Yesterday at a grocery store in San Marino, in a moment of what-the-hellness, I bought two wooden utensils, ideal for turning scrambled eggs on the nonstick pan we bought down in Rimini last week. They will join my mother-in-law's collection of wooden spoons in the drawer over here. I've used one of my new pieces already. It's just what I needed, or rather, just what I *wanted*. (The difference between need and want is often difficult to unblur.) It takes years to season a wooden spoon. The ones I just bought are smooth and blonde; those in the drawer are dark, stained by decades of olive oil and meat fat and tomato, nicked and pitted from use. They are historical spoons.

Someday someone will have to open the drawers and empty them. I'm thinking about that, about zones of economy and excess, what I can and want to do, what I *should* do about stuff.

Who needs forty-nine beach towels?

Who needs twenty-six bill caps?

Who needs dozens of screwdrivers and wooden spoons?

Who needs an anvil?

Some of our stuff we just *want*. It's how we know we are ourselves. It's a reminder of where we've been, where we come from; a reminder of those we loved and those who loved us.

# 22

# Try a Little BLT

"PLEASE BRING A SPRAY bottle of melatonin."

It's the day before we leave for Shanghai. My daughter is sending I forgot messages. I forgot Gabriel's swim goggles. I forgot to pack the new baby monitor. I forgot the fenugreek capsules. Her tone is apologetic. She knows she's adding to the anxiety of our pretrip prep. In her WeChat message this morning, however, you can sense low-level desperation.

It's the Please.

"Please, bring a spray bottle of melatonin."

I've already packed three-milligram tablets. I tell her that.

"Please. It has to be spray. The boys' jet lag is killing us."

Please.

Ah, sleep. Sayeth Macbeth, It knits up the ravell'd sleave of care. When kids can't sleep no one sleeps.

The time difference between Detroit and Shanghai is thirteen hours. You have to cross the International Date Line. That will turn your world upside down. It's day for night. Plus you lose a day.

The IDL was discovered inadvertently by Ferdinand Magellan when he circumnavigated the globe. Upon return in 1519 he realized he'd lost a day. The Italian historian Antonio Pigafetta chronicled the Portuguese explorer's discovery, noting:

*The Spanyardes hauynge sayled abowt three yeares and one moneth, and the most of them notynge the dayes, day by day (as is the maner of all them that sayle by the Ocean) they founde when they were returned to Spayne, that they had loste one day. So that at theyr arryuall at the porte of Siuile [Seville] beinge the seventh day of September, was by theyr accompt but the sixth day.*

I've never lost a day. A few nights perhaps. But never a day. Not like this.

Our plan is to spend one night in LA with our son, then fly out of LAX the next day. The time difference between Detroit and Los Angeles is three hours. Rather than flying fourteen hours and losing the day (still difficult to comprehend) and facing the big lag in Shanghai all at once, we'll ease into the new time zone, beginning with minor lag in LA. It just might work.

Except it won't. And, really, there's no such thing as minor lag. Lag is lag.

Furthermore, it won't work because of the way I sleep. And don't. I wake up early every day. My new time to rise: 4:00 a.m. Detroit time. I've formed a habit. More than a habit, it has become a lifestyle. So in LA I expect to be awake at 1:00 a.m. What will that be, 10:00 a.m. in Shanghai? Wherever I am I will be awake at the wrong time.

My friend Rob goes to China on business—more often than seems humanly possible.

"You want to know how to avoid jet lag?" he says a few days before we leave.

"Yes," I tell him, "I want to avoid it. Or at least minimize it."

"First, you avoid coffee two days before departure."

"How would that be possible?"

"And alcohol for two days before departure."

"Possibly even more impossible."

"Listen," he says, "this works. Two days, no caffeine, no alcohol. Then after you board you immediately go to sleep as soon as the plane takes off. Do you have a noise-cancelling headset?"

"Yes."

"Do you have a sleep mask?"

"Who doesn't?" No, I don't. But I think Delta usually hands them out.

"Don't eat the dinner."

"And don't drink the drink, I assume."

"Right."

He says you sleep as long as you can. When you wake up you have three cups of coffee. Really get yourself caffeinated. And you'll need exposure to light. "I like to go the back of the plane," he says, "pull open the shade, and just stand there, looking into the sun."

It pleases me, somehow, to think of Rob staring at the sun. He would be smiling. "For how long?"

"You'll have seven or eight more hours to fly. Soak up the light. Watch movies, read. Enjoy yourself. Go look at the sun. When you get to Shanghai it's evening. Get to the hotel. Go to bed."

We'll be checking in on the grandchildren, sleepless in Shanghai, and their bleary parents. So going to bed is unlikely.

Anyway I contemplate this strategy late at night at my son's house when we reach LA.

Note to self: When you spend the night in a strange house locate the light switches before you go to bed.

True to form I wake up at 1:00 a.m. Force myself to stay in bed another hour or so. When I can't lie still any longer I stumble into the living room where, along with everywhere else in the house, it's dark. On the kitchen stove the digital display reads 2:30. On the kitchen counter I know there is an espresso machine. I figure: Why not?

Another note to self: before you go to bed at night locate the coffee can for the next morning.

Kitchens are tricky. I look for light switches, take a chance on one next to a door figuring it's safe, far enough from the sink. I flip the switch and of course the garbage disposal comes to life. In the dead of night its metallic whine is deafening. I give up on the coffee, take a seat in the living room, read daytime WeChat messages from the exhausted ones in Shanghai. An hour or so after I get up I hear a helicopter roaring across the sky. It seems to hover in the near distance, where it must be low, reminding me of the Los Angeles helicopters in Robert Altman's *Short Cuts*. Or was it William Friedkin's *To Live and Die in LA*? Life is mysterious at 3:00 a.m.

There's a name for what I do, for my condition: advanced sleep phase syndrome. (Some researchers refer to it as a disorder. I prefer syndrome.) According to the National Sleep Foundation: "The sleep rhythm is shifted forward so that 7 or 8 hours of sleep are still obtained but the individuals will wake up extremely early because they have gone to sleep quite early."

That's me, all right, except for the seven or eight hours part. I'm five or six. On a good night, six and a quarter or six and a half hours.

Recent research reported in the journal *Neuron* suggests I may be stuck with abbreviated sleep and slugfests with jet lag. As you age certain mechanisms in the brain go on the fritz. I will never again sleep till noon, except maybe this week in Shanghai, which is unlikely.

Matthew Walker, a sleep and neuroimaging expert at the University of California, Berkeley, notes, "Evolutionarily, sleep is about the dumbest thing you would ever do." (Along with using "evolution" as an adverb.) Asleep, he observes, you are at your most vulnerable. You're not hunting and gathering, or looking after your kids, or keeping a lookout for predators. It may be evolutionarily dumb, but sleep we must.

The syndrome is treated with BLT. No kidding. But not *that* BLT. (I wish.) The solution is Bright Light Therapy. There's a bright light box, a bright light visor. These devices help tune your suprachiasmatic nuclei and by association your circadian rhythms.

Which is why Rob drinks in the sun at the back of the plane. Sousing his suprachiasmatic nuclei. Reprogramming his circadian rhythms.

I might try it. But in these matters I am not an optimist. We'll all be stuck in jet lag unless melatonin in whatever form (mist, tablet, cocktail) delivers us. I can only hope.

# 23

# And Then You Eat It

HELLO. THANK YOU.

So far that's all the Chinese I know. *Nihao* (KNEE-how). *Xiexie* (sheh-sheh).

I could use one more word right away: fork.

Coming to Shanghai I knew I would face the challenge of how to get food in my mouth. I'll use chopsticks in restaurants back home. It's kind of fun for about five minutes. I adjust my grip and the length of the sticks, align them, and go for the pinch and lift. When my grasp fails I stab whatever I can with one stick and take comfort in knowing there is always a fallback plan, a life preserver. Flatware. Inevitably I'll lay my chopsticks down so I can pick up a fork and fully engage the food.

I should have youtubed chopstick technique before I left. I should have practiced.

For our inaugural dining experience here, the kids take us to a place called Fu 1088. The restaurant is a three-story Spanish-style mansion in what was once Shanghai's International Settlement. You call, make a reservation, and upon arrival are shown to your own private dining room. It's just you, a big lazy Susan, and in short order a lot of food. And chopsticks.

Fortunately this night we start with bamboo soup (I ladle slippery bamboo pith mouthward, my first time eating pith), which means I get a spoon. I make a point of keeping it. Next comes grilled eel, a noodle dish, hairy crab meat (*What?*), fresh river shrimp, fried rice, braised pork with soy and rock sugar, pumpkin dumplings, a dish of dumplings full of hot broth, a dish of green beans, something else with lychee nuts. When the server is not in the room I set down one chopstick and push food onto the spoon with the other. I see my wife doing likewise.

"Hold them higher," my daughter says. She shows me her stickwork.

I think I get the physics—long sticks, more force transferred to the tips and to the foodstuff. The problem is that it's fine motor at a distance. Robotic surgery at the dinner table.

I try my sticks a little higher.

"There you go," she says."

I lower them to a green bean. No go.

"It's all in the thumb."

It probably is. Just not my thumb.

Okay, I could just say, "你有没有叉子" Or show the server that sentence on my phone. Or I could say, Nǐ yǒu méiyǒu chāzi?? If I could say that. The active ingredient in both sentences being 叉子 and chāzi, the word for fork.

I could ask for a fork, but I don't. It's sort of a matter of pride. And, well, fair play. Back home you don't see Chinese tourists asking for chopsticks at Denny's or Ponderosa.

Street food is much more hands-on. It's a delivery system I understand and mastered a long time ago. On our way to breakfast the next morning, a Saturday, on every block there are eight or ten storefronts with clouds of steam rising from vats and tandoor ovens. Outside these places people in line wait for the goods. We stop twice to eat.

At the first place we wait for barrel bread with mushrooms and pork. A few feet inside a double door that opens onto the sidewalk, a skinny man in a white apron and billcap rolls out dough, daubs mushroom mix or pork bits on it, and presses the bread to the side of the tandoor oven. The results are revelatory.

At the next stop we have scallion pancakes: just-in-time crepes with an egg broken and slathered over them and cooked, along with hoisin sauce and scallions and a crunchy fried bread stick. The chef is a young guy. He looks well fed. He folds the crepe, slices it, wraps it in tissue paper, and hands it over.

My wife eats. I know that look on her face. "We're coming back here," she says.

"There are hundreds of places like this in Shanghai," my son-in-law says. "Probably thousands." Indeed.

My wife says nothing. She doesn't need to. Or is temporarily indisposed as she reckons with her crepe.

I picture that mountain of mushroom mix and the bowl of diced pork at the first stand and think about Shanghai summer. "Do you ever wonder," I say to my daughter, "about, you know, hygiene?"

"I didn't eat this stuff when I was pregnant," she says. "But it's so good."

I picture the local chapter of the Shanghai Health Department, its office in a garage down at the end of an alley. CNN *Travel* reports that Shanghai has more than ten thousand local food stalls. An investigation in 2011 of chuan (cooked foods) on eleven streets in Shanghai found that 609 of the 650 street vendors had no license. "Only 30 percent of the city's street food had reliable ingredient sources," the *Shanghai Evening Post* reported. In the CNN article there's a link to another article, "Shanghai Cracks Down on Toxic Hot Pots." I choose not to read this article. Where ignorance is bliss . . .

"It's pretty simple," my son-in-law says. "I look for a line. If there's no line I don't eat there."

It's an indication of how hungry she is, and how good the food tastes, that my wife eats this street food at all. Visiting our son in Manhattan we walked by a gazillion kebab carts, along with pizza, kwik meat, empanada, memela, tortilla and taco, gourmet grilled cheese, French fry, pretzel, waffle, noodle, barbecue, sausage and schnitzel, and hot dog stands. She could be starving and would still walk past them without blinking an eye. I don't eat street food, she would say.

When we got to Shanghai I expected her to say No xiexie.

The next day we have lunch at a Yunnan restaurant. The cuisine is southwestern Chinese, my son-in-law says, spicy, famous for its mashed potatoes and mushrooms. I try longsticking everything on the table with limited success. Mashed potatoes, I'm happy to find, are chopstick accessible. Feeling very conspicuous I backslide occasionally to my chopstick-drag-and-spoon method and get through the meal. At the next table is a family of five. Their stick skills are impressive. One guy I watch could probably reach into his pocket, jingle the coins, find and extract a penny.

"Pass the potatoes," I say to my wife, wondering about the incidence of carpal tunnel syndrome among chopstick amateurs.

"I really think you're getting it," my daughter says. I grab a glob and eat.

# 24

# Buddy, Can You Spare a Mao?

IN FEBRUARY IT'S COLD in Shanghai.

The week we arrive James comes to our apartment twice to help us regulate the heat. One morning I wake up feeling like a steamed dumpling; in the afternoon of the same day I layer up in the living room, trying to keep warm. When we call the desk downstairs, in five minutes James appears at the door. He is thin, dressed in black pants and the property company blazer. He looks like he's in his late twenties, medium height, with a shock of black hair and black glasses. He kicks off his shoes and goes to the thermostat. His English is pretty good, though he's a more fluent speaker than listener. When I see him around the building he's always in a hurry. We say hello to each other now.

One day I get on the elevator and there he is, going down.

*Nihao, James.* I smile, then turn away.

James is holding a huge pile of pink banknotes, a stack four inches high. I was taught there are a few things you don't talk about in public, sex and money for example. James has his hand clamped around a lot of money. I don't say anything; it would not be polite to look. Maybe the Chinese are okay with displays of cash, the way some cultures are cool with nudity.

And maybe it's not that much money.

Before coming to Shanghai I really should have studied up a little more on money and money etiquette.

Here is a defining image of the feckless tourist: poking at strange coins cupped in his hand, thumbing through assorted bills on a street corner or, worse, in front of a cash register. *How much is this? I'm holding a fifty. But fifty what? Is that a lot or a little?*

MONEY MATTERS ARE NEVER easy at first.

For tourists China is pretty much a cash economy. Learning the money is an urgent matter. You expect to pay cash for chicken feet on the street, but at the Nike store? Your Visa card is useless. Don't bother leaving home with your American Express. And unlike Europe, where ATM's are all over the place, here they are rare, and most of them will not accept your Bank of America ATM card.

Second day we're here my son-in-law takes me to the Bank of China a few blocks from the apartment. There are four ATM machines, only one equipped with English.

"Get the max," he says.

"That's three thousand." It seems a lot. Or is it?

Chinese money is called RMB, short for renminbi, which means "people's currency." It's also called CNY, which is short for Chinese yuan. One Chinese yuan equals about fifteen cents. The yuan is broken down into ten jiao, sometimes called "mao," and the jiao is broken down into ten fen. Buddy, can you spare a mao?

Gradually I get a handle on things, though in passing I keep referring to RMBs as RBIs (I always wanted a lot of RBIs).

At Bank of China I enter my PIN number, press Enter, and the machine chatters for a few seconds. When it stops I pull out my three thousand RBIs in thirty crisp pink C-notes, which I fold and shove deep in my pants pocket. I do the math. About $450. At home I never walk around with that much cash on me.

With that wad in my pocket I think, of course, about being mugged.

On the flight over I sat next to a woman whose husband works in Shanghai. They take turns shuttling back and forth between LA and Shanghai. I was awake the whole flight while she wore a mask, wrapped herself in a scarf, and slept. Upon landing she turned to me and asked what brought me to Shanghai. We chatted a minute.

I asked her how safe Shanghai is.

"Very safe," she said. "You can be on the street late at night without fear. Even the single woman."

"Crime?"

"No," she said. "Crime is not a problem. The real danger is traffic."

So true.

In short order I learn that I could easily get run over with those C-notes in my pocket.

THE HIGH-RISE OUR KIDS live in is on a one-way street. There are a lot of one-way streets in Shanghai, most of them with bike lanes that go in both directions on either side of the road. Perhaps the one-way street is part of the city's traffic management program. On these streets you find cars, trucks, motorcycles, electric motor scooters, electric bicycles, electric bicycle trucks, conventional bicycle trucks, and conventional bicycles. Look both ways when you step off the sidewalk. Look very, very carefully. Whatever is coming at you is likely to be electric or foot-powered and whisper quiet.

Traffic is dense and by law very, very quiet, thanks to an official crackdown on horns and parking and bad manners. In an interview with *Sixth Tone: Fresh Voices from Today's China*, Wei Kairen, a former deputy head of traffic police, comments on Shanghai's "big traffic overhaul." It's all about helping implement policies to "keep the city's traffic situation civilized." She adds, "We have established and enforced 'no-blaring zones' and clamped down on illegal horn use. Even though it might seem like a small act, this kind of behavior is uncivilized and encourages road rage." It's against the law here, evidently, to be inconsiderate.

In this city of bicycles an experiment is under way to make the city even more bicycle friendly. On the sidewalks, parked and ready, are blue, yellow, orange, and red dockless bikes; according to a recent count as many as half a million of them. There are so many dockless bikes, along with the privately-owned bikes and scooters parked on the sidewalk, that pedestrians are often forced into the street, where you can be very quietly run over. (Then again you can be quietly run over on the sidewalk, too, as electric motor scooter, electric bicycle, and conventional bicycle riders are not disinclined to use the sidewalk when it's convenient.)

I contemplate taking a dockless bike for a spin when traffic is at low tide, maybe on a Sunday morning at six o'clock. They cost ¥0.5 to ¥1 for a thirty-minute ride. I just might do that, but I can't. There is no way to pay for one. Mobike, Ofo, Bluegogo, Xiaoming, and Coolqi do not take credit cards. Forget cash. Bluegogo and all the others are a no-go unless you have WeChat or Alipay, apps that are connected to your Chinese bank account.

Which brings us back to money.

If I rode a Bluegogo bike for a couple hours, what would that really cost? How many yuan for that? And what's that in dollars?

Every day here I am faced with story problems like that.

And like this:

Rick is up early and would like a cappuccino. He walks to Bread Etc., takes a seat, and orders coffee. If one yuan equals $.15 U.S., and a cappuccino costs RMB 30, how much does Rick pay for his cappuccino?

And this:

Rick is hungry for fresh fruit. He goes to a Shanghai vegetable market to buy fruit. He buys six bananas for RMB 16, four apples, and a kilo of brown rice for RMB 28. When he gets to the cash register the cashier rings up his apples twice, two for RMB 38. What is the total cost of these groceries in RMB? In U.S. dollars, how much does Rick pay for his groceries? (Extra credit: calculate the cost per apple in U.S. dollars. State your opinion: Are apples expensive in China? Support your answer by referring to your calculations.)

Every day is fraught with moments like these.

One solution is to cast your cares to the wind and just pass one of your C-notes over the counter, even if you're buying one item, like a pack of AA batteries. Outside the store you stand contemplating your receipt, doing the after-the-fact math. *What, only* RMB *17 for ten batteries? That's $2.55 for batteries. What a great deal!*

On the other hand, if you're keen on monitoring your expenses and not appearing like a dunce to the cashier, you try to do the math before you get to the register. A baguette is RMB 15, which, let's see, is $2.25. Not bad. Doing this saves you the grief of standing at the cash register and being told in Chinese, repeatedly, how many RBIs you need to hand over.

A couple days ago I went to the FMart next door for a liter of milk. I made the mistake of not looking at the price and doing the math beforehand. The cashier took the bottle, rang it up, told me what I owed.

I handed her a ten-RMB note.

She shook her head.

I reached in my pocket and handed her a bunch of coins, nodding the nod that says, in English anyway, *take the money you need so I can get out of here.*

She looked at the coins, shook her head, and handed them back. She repeated herself in Chinese, telling me what I owed quite a bit louder than before, and gave me the look: Blockhead. Behind me there was a long line. At the next two registers were equally long lines.

I pulled out a few more bills from my pocket. *Let's see, I have tens and twenties. How much could milk possibly cost?* Forgetting that ten is not ten, really, in China. It's actually $1.50. Once more she asked for more money. I handed her another ten-RBI note and she gave me back a few coins (yuan or jiao or mao or fen), and I was out of there.

It was peak rush hour on the street. The sidewalk was crowded. I walked carefully back to the apartment, wishing I could be a little less feckless.

# 25

# The Dope with the Camera

THIS MORNING I TOOK a picture of my breakfast. I didn't do it to remember it. I took the picture with sharing in mind.

We've come to Bread Etc. five consecutive mornings. It's a French place—baguettes, pastries, Edith Piaf singing "Chanson d'Amour" on the sound system the last three mornings—in the French Concession area of Shanghai, near our kids' apartment. Bread Etc. is a knife-and-fork establishment. There's not a dumpling or chopstick in sight.

Here they speak Chinese, not French, so ordering has been a struggle. (Even with enthusiastic pantomime it took a while to explain jam, do you have jam, we would like jam for our bread-that's-almost-toast.) But every morning the Chinese waitkids dressed in their blue untucked gingham shirts and navy chinos smile and wave at us, *Hello, good morning,* and the manager has now saved our order on her iPad. Farmer's omelet for the lady (no dressing on the salad, no butter on the toast, no salami in the omelet—try to picture the pantomime it took to explain all *that*), avocado sandwich for the gentleman.

I'm not sure anyone saw me take a picture of my sandwich. Not that anyone would care. And not that anyone would care to see it either. My picture-taking, like most people's these days, is wanton, an example of ordinary excess.

These images are souvenirs. The clothes hung out to dry above a storefront; on the same line, next to shirts and undies, three large eels, also drying. The London plane trees that line the streets in the French Concession, more than a hundred years old, cropped and pruned, their bark blotchy and peeling, so like the sycamores we see on Via Tripoli and Via Pascoli in Rimini. (By now I've stood in the middle of Xiangyang Road ten times or more, at various hours of the day, in various slants of light, trying to capture the look and feel of those trees.)

More souvenirs: I want to take home the storefront signs, with their odd use of English. Fashion Warm Pants. Urban Jungle Real Estate. Food Fun Delivered. Seewant. King Man Spa. Flower Fingers. Gag Story. Beast Tattoo. I want to remember faces. The man mending shoes on the sidewalk (he waved me off—no photo). The man at the foot-powered sewing machine on the sidewalk (he waved me off—no photo). The man slicing open and cleaning a huge eel (he said yes!). The hundreds of people in front of the Wanhua Tower in the Yu Yuan Garden, with hundreds of cameras seeing the sights before the seers.

THE UBIQUITOUS CAMERA. How does it alter the moment of perception? Does it absent the viewer from the fullness of experience?

Years ago, when our kids were small and went to birthday parties, the video camera was just making its first appearance. It was a machine about the size of a microwave oven that dads rested on their shoulders while shouting directions at children. *Sit down! Darcy, stand behind Tanya! Blow out the candles! Now! Blow!* Lights, camera, action! I remember thinking: These dopes, they're not really here. They won't see the party until they get home and turn on the TV.

Walker Percy, in an essay called "Loss of Creature," pokes fun at the American tourist who goes to the Grand Canyon, measuring its beauty against countless postcard and poster and brochure and television images he has seen. If it looks like the postcard, Percy says, "[the tourist] is pleased; he might even say, 'Why it is every bit as beautiful as a picture postcard!' He feels he has not been cheated. But if it does not conform, if the colors are somber, he will not be able to see it directly; he will only be conscious of the disparity between what it is and what it is supposed to be."

In *On Photography* Susan Sontag echoes this idea: "Photography is the reality; the real object is often experienced as a letdown." As if anticipating the cell phone and its camera and today's take-a-picture madness, Sontag remarks on the "insatiability of the photographing eye."

Oh yes.

A few Sundays ago we took the kids to the Shanghai aquarium, said to be the largest in Asia. It's big. And do they have the water creatures: arapaima gigas, lepidosirens, electric eels, freshwater sawfishes, archerfishes, and the famous melanotaenia maccullochi; cichlids, thiania subopressa, green water dragons, osphronemus goramy, and a few exotic species like the bluegill (no kidding).

At eleven o'clock there was already a crowd. At every display the locals pressed themselves to the glass, small children holding cell phones to take underwater pictures and video, not-so-small children holding cell phones to take surface level pictures and video, adults holding cell phones to capture, from their altitude, more global pictures and video of the display. Nowhere have I ever seen such an orgy of picture taking.

The exotic will do that to you. You want to capture it, to save it.

ON A DAILY BASIS since our arrival I've felt like an exotic species. Walking down the sidewalk we get the look. It lasts a second or two. At home we are ordinary as bluegills. Not here. The look lasts just a moment longer than normal. *You're not from around here.* Then every so often on the same sidewalk, because this is an international place, we see someone that, well, looks like us.

It reminds me of when our kids were small. When my wife and I went to watch them play little league baseball there was always a mom and dad who brought the family dog to watch Steven or Katie knock one out of the infield. The dog sat leashed in the bleachers, bored to tears, waiting for someone, anyone, to hit a foul ball. Inevitably another mom and dad would show up with their dog, let it loose, and the two animals would just go bonkers. They were surrounded by humans, lonely in the isolation of their dogless situation, when, suddenly, another one of their own species appeared. *Hey, you're one of us.* An ecstasy of eager dog diplomacy would ensue, circling and sniffing, licking and nipping.

On the sidewalk in Shanghai we are the dogs. Suddenly we look up and, with surprise and pleasure, we see another Westerner. *Look, a French poodle!* Or, *Here comes a German shepherd!* Or, *Hey, that guy might be an Alaskan huskie!*

You get used to the look, to being foreign. Sometimes, however, the locals lose it. Particularly when they see a Western child. Kathy Flower, a British radio and television producer, observes in *China—Culture Smart*, "Westerners traveling with their children will find them the center of attention. It can be a bit overwhelming for very young Western children to have their cheeks pinched and their arms stroked almost beyond endurance. They may have to pose for endless selfies." This is not an exaggeration, and it's no joke.

One day our daughter is stopped on the sidewalk by a young woman who gapes at our grandson and asks, in pretty good English, if her friends can take a picture of him *with her*. Our daughter is about to say no when the boy, feeling surprised and flattered, says yes. The girl claps an arm around his shoulder and hauls him close. He freezes, totally weirded out, if not terrified, a wooden smile on his face. A few days later at the Yu Garden, seeing our three-year-old, a woman squeals with delight and rushes toward him, lowering herself to his level. *My God,* I think, *she's going to hug him.* When she holds out her arms I turn him away from her (he already senses the impending assault) and tell her no. More like: *No!* You wait, fully expecting, *How about a selfie with him, then?*

In the next few minutes I notice a camera with a giant telephoto lens following us, a man aiming at our boy. No.

The camera lens is more invasive, more penetrating than the eye. Stares are not cool. The shutter clicks open and shut like a trap.

These are not mean or terrible people. Far from it. They are simply not mindful of boundaries (nor am I at times), and I have every reason to think it has to do with the device they hold in their hands, a technology that makes every interesting thing in sight (fair, curly-haired three-year-old American child; waitkid dressed in blue, untucked gingham shirt and navy chinos; stooped, arthritic shoe repairman on the sidewalk) into an object one would enjoy capturing, saving, and sharing.

Before we leave Shanghai we will go to the Long Museum to see a Rembrandt exhibit. If photos are permitted I'll have my iPhone cocked and ready, my finger on the trigger. I like to photograph faces; I like to look for small details in the corner or bottom of paintings, the eels on the clothesline. Camerawise I won't be alone. In gallery visits these days we always have to wait for people to photograph a painting before we can get close to it. Why take pictures of paintings? Why not just *look* at them? Maybe I'm not fully present. Maybe this is secondary seeing, not as rich and full and satisfying as unmediated viewing.

A recent study by the American Psychological Association suggests otherwise, arguing that taking pictures might even enhance our experience—of a Rembrandt, a street corner in Shanghai, or an avocado sandwich. The researchers, Kristin Diehl, PhD, of the University of Southern California; Gal Zauberman, PhD, of Yale University; and Alixandra Barasch, PhD, of the University of Pennsylvania, contend, "Relative to not taking photos, photography can heighten enjoyment of positive experiences by increasing engagement."

A secondary question: Must we share? Thanks to social media we are profligate in this regard, some people more than others. Okay, the pleasure I take in my avocado sandwich is enhanced, maybe a tiny bit, by my taking its picture. But restraint is called for. I should keep it to myself. Take a bite, savor and swallow, leave it at that.

# 26

# ATM, Wontons, Lizard

AFTER THE JET LAG passes (it takes a week) I'm getting up again at five o'clock every morning. No, I *want* to get up that early. Everyone has their quiet time. This is mine.

One morning I shuffle in bare feet into the kitchen to make coffee. There are two small children in the apartment. For the love of God, let them sleep a few more hours. Every sound is deafening: the tick of a spoon on the kitchen counter, the spray and percussion of water in the sink, the sticky refrigerator door that goes *thonk* when I pull it open. Back in the living room I foolishly decide to put my pants on while standing up, in the dark. What could be a perfunctory operation goes badly. With both legs pushing into the same pant leg, I lose my balance and tip over sideways, flopping with a silent splash onto the couch. Unhurt.

This instance of clutzery is a metaphor for my life in Shanghai up to this point.

Later this morning I leave the apartment in search of a China Construction Bank ATM. It's been a while since I've been able to get any cash. In five days of very inconvenient calls to Bank of America (go ahead, just try to use one of those toll-free international numbers on the back of your card), I've been assured no problem, my account is now unlocked. No, it's not. Most recently Mark in Albuquerque, the supervisor I ask for, insists with profuse apologies that he sees my account is definitely unlocked now, and please be sure to use China Construction Bank to avoid fees. I find the location of a number of branch offices on my phone, map three of them within a mile of the apartment. I'm pretty sure I know where I'm going.

On the corner where there's supposed to be a China Construction Bank I find Zhong Hua Beef Noodles. I walk a little further, to a wide driveway guarded by four cops. It's a school entrance. I nod *Hello, I'm looking for a bank*, trying not to look like a child molester.

At a coffee bar nearby I order coffee, get back online to locate another bank branch, snap a picture of the map on my phone. I walk off in this new direction. Passing Shanghai Culture Square, it occurs to me that I can't ask anyone for directions. You can't, under almost any circumstances, say, "Do you know where——is?" when you can't even say "——."

The map I screen-captured is borderline useless, but somehow I find my way to the bank. It's a big branch that, judging from the leaves and grime, has been dead for quite a while. The letters spelling the bank's name have been stripped off the building, leaving sooty silhouettes of both the Chinese and English characters. The ATM cabin at the side of building is locked. Above the cabin is a sign, China Construction Bank, 建设银行. In a moment of inspiration I take a picture of the sign above the ATM so I can show someone.

Ten minutes later, at the crosswalk on another street corner, I show this photo to a man holding a briefcase. He looks at me, mildly irritated, then glances at my phone. In a blink he points south. I smile and say *xiexie*, one of my two words in Chinese, thinking as I do: I've already been to the branch in that direction, and was declined five times at the ATM. I do not want to revisit failure. I also think: *How in the world did he read that sign so fast?* When I look at traditional Chinese characters I see chopsticks and noodles. But then, of course, the man can read Chinese.

Chopsticks and noodles: a quick study (which is no study at all) tells me Chinese characters consist of pictographs and glyphs, ideograms and compound ideographs. There are thirty thousand characters. A functionally literate person would require three thousand or so to read a newspaper.

The character for bank is 銀行.

I heard it said that once you can read a word you can't *not* read it when you see it. Perception and [re]cognition are instantaneous. It's a reminder of how tremendously enabling and empowering literacy is. When you can read you live in the midst of things, people, and processes, as well as signs and symbols. You are embedded in signification and meaning. The inability to decode even the most ordinary language renders much of the world unintelligible. You are surrounded by people and things and processes and a lot of silent gibberish.

Here, for all intents and purposes, I am an illiterate deaf-mute. Photographs are my lifeline.

Early one afternoon my daughter and I have wonton soup in a diner a few blocks from the apartment. This outing is one part austerity program—I'm still under the Bank of America curse— one part enjoy agenda. We get two large bowls of soup and beer for RMB 30, about five bucks. The soup is delicious, huge wontons with a meaty, greeny filling. In the five booths on one side of the restaurant and the one long table down the middle of the narrow room, with stools on either side, the place can seat forty people. We take a couple stools.

At one point she looks up from her bowl and says, "I want that next time."

Next to her, his face lowered to his food, a guy is lifting noodles and a large cutlet from a bowl of dark broth. Of course she can't say, What's that? She pulls out her phone, raises it, and offers the universal gesture: *Can I take a picture of what you're eating?*

He sets down his chopsticks, a blank look on his face, leans back so she can get a clean shot.

"What's the name of this place?" I ask her.

"I don't know." Danny, her husband, found it.

There are joints back home simply called Eat. I make a note to look that character up, strictly for the fun of it. It would please me if, next time we walked by, I could match the characters. Eat.

On our way out we stop at the register, where there's a stack of menus, most of them one-page lists, all in Chinese. A few of them are compendious multipage books, with large color photos of the food and writing next to the photos, none of it in English. The thing to do, I guess, is take pictures of the pictures so as not to bother a guy eating noodles and cutlet.

I look for a business card. Forget about it. Besides, what am I going to do, call for carryout?

Somehow the cashier gets the message and writes on my daughter's phone: Cheng Huang Miao Chi. That's a lot of words. Could it be Eat at Chou's? Back in the apartment I run it through my Google Translate. I get "Cheng Huang MI AO C Hi" Hi!

TripAdvisor has a listing for the restaurant. The title of the first review is "Do Not Eat Here."

FLUSH WITH CASH FROM the China Construction Bank branch I eventually find, I buy our three-year-old a toy lizard. It's green, eight inches long, battery operated. According to the instructions, which, miraculously, are provided in both Chinese and English, and which I have read very carefully, when you remove the screws from the lizard's belly the battery door should open. Use two AA batteries. We have a Phillips-head screwdriver. It's the wrong size, but four screws come out when I carefully insist. Whereupon two problems emerge. One, these are odd Chinese screws, with three-point heads (if I insist too much I'll ruin the screwheads), and two, there's a fifth screw, sunk deeper in the lizard than the others.

Sitting at the kitchen table I read the directions again, a couple times, cursing the fifth screw. Standing at my elbow the three-year-old watches, waits.

It's the fifth screw, I tell him. We need a long narrow three-point screwdriver.

Can you fix it?

I'll have to go out and buy a screwdriver.

My wife suggests I bring the lizard with me, so I can show the person what the problem is. Provide some context.

I picture myself walking down the sidewalk holding a green lizard. There are much weirder sights out here, I know that, but I decide to keep it simple.

*Screwdriver. Hardware store.* I look these words up on Google translate and take their picture.

Man with the sewing machine is fixing a jacket zipper. He doesn't even look up. I stand in front of him almost a full minute. He must see my legs and feet. I can't say "excuse me." Finally I carefully lower my left hand, with a tiny three-point screw pinched between my thumb and forefinger, into his field of vision and pantomime the universal motion of a man removing a screw from a mechanical green lizard.

He stops and looks at the screw, he glances up at me, he shakes his head. No.

And goes back to the zipper.

I would like to say, "I'm sorry to be such a pain in the ass," but I can't. I hate to do it, but I pull out my phone and carefully thrust it into his field of vision, showing him the screen and the words I've photographed.

He shakes his head again. No. As in no, I don't know where there's a hardware store, or no, I've told you no twice now and I don't have time for your shenanigans. Or possibly no, I can't read. I hope for option B.

The shoe repair man working his section of the sidewalk reads the words and points to the end of the block. Turn right. At least that's what I think he says. The fruit stand man on the corner reads the words and says, no, you have to go left. I go left.

The toy store man reads the words and says go to the right at the next corner.

I find not one but two hardware stores. The man at the second one I visit immediately decodes my screwdriver pantomime. He looks at the screwhead, smiles, and holds up three fingers. He produces the item. The screwdriver costs more than two bowls of wonton soup and a beer, but I'll take it. I hand him the necessary R M B. I have a whole pocketful of them. I scored at the bank.

Back home we will have a very happy three-year old. And I'm feeling pretty good too.

Hello. Thank you.

Nihao. Xiexie.

# 27

# Fang Xin

"IF I LIVED HERE," I tell my daughter, "I would shop at Fart Mart."

I'm referring to the grocery store next to the high-rise where she'll be living the next two years or so. Its real name is FMart. She goes there only when she has to.

FMart is a full-service grocery store with a Chinese accent. The store combines elements of industrial food production and distribution with the traditional Chinese "wet market." It's about the size of a large 7–Eleven, well, four 7–Elevens piled on top of each other. Four floors of pure pandemonium.

Wet? If you picture a farmer's market such as you would find in the United States, you're almost there. Now add meat and fish, stir in some poultry, and you have a wet market. Wet means everything uncovered, unwrapped, naked, and exposed to the human touch, minus the sanitary precautions required in the handling and sale of meat and fish in the U.S. Looking for chicken breasts? There's a pile of them on that table over there. Go ahead and pick up a few, find the ones you want. How about some pork ribs? There are stacks of them not far from the chicken, right next to the duck carcasses. Grab a few and take a look. Find the slab that's right for you. Thinking about eel for dinner tonight? No, I didn't think so. But if you are, they've got dried eels, recently eviscerated eels on ice, and live eels crammed in a tank. Pinch a few. Take your pick. You were looking for something different? How about some nice purple duck?

On walks I've taken since arriving in Shanghai, a few blocks from here I've seen similar stores, with names like Family Mart and Fresh Mart. The *F* in FMart might be short for one of those more wholesome adjectives.

I don't know about those stores, but deep inside our FMart, where all the raw meat and seafood and poultry can be found, where all the *wet* is, the atmosphere is aromatic in the extreme.

Hence the nickname.

THE FIRST MEAL HONG, the new nanny, cooks for us is almost all fresh vegetables. I'm not sure of the source. Carrot and celery in a sauce that tastes, well, Chinese; boiled broccoli, sautéed spinach, and a cabbage dish with something orange mixed in it.

"What is this?" I ask my daughter, inspecting a chunk of the orange stuff.

She says it's egg.

Of course, egg. I like egg.

Hong's food is good. Very good. In an act of public relations genius she gives the three-year-old a pair of starter chopsticks. He inserts his fingers and thumb into strategically positioned rings, assumes perfect stick form. There's no fumbling, little droppage. Pleased with how competent he is, especially compared to my wife and me (we could benefit from a pair of starters ourselves), he eats everything on his plate. Including, of course, the egg. And asks for more.

I've seen eggs at FMart and in baskets the size of milk crates in the neighborhood food stalls. I make a mental note to ask my daughter, Where did those eggs come from?

The Chinese love their eggs. Eggs are integral to their cuisine. In a city of twenty-four million egg lovers you can't help but pause and wonder at the challenge, the miracle, and the health implications of making tens of millions of eggs available to consumers every day, seven days a week.

It stands to reason that China is the biggest egg producer in the world. Compassion in World Farming estimates production at over 450 billion eggs a year. That's twenty million tons of eggs laid by

2.7 billion hens. *The Journal of Food Protection* reports that Chinese egg-inspection standards, needed to watch for heavy metals, veterinary drugs, and micro-organisms in eggs, are a little squishy.

When I ask later, my daughter says Hong used the eggs she bought at City Super, Shanghai's Whole Foods, where everything is a whole lot more expensive, a store fully evolved into the Western model, by which I mean dry.

Next afternoon Hong and I are in the kitchen together. I'm making a big pot of bean soup. It's my second soup since we got here, a food that connects us to our point of origin and restoreth the soul. The first one, pre-Hong, I made with adzuki beans I bought at FMart. Same recipe as home except for the beans, which make a deep brown broth. It was a good soup. The five of us ate all of it in one sitting. When I tell my wife I'm making soup again, and how about the FMart adzukis, she frowns. She says she doesn't like brown food. (I know this.) She wants a nice clear soup, with a light broth, so that the vegetables are visible. FMart, I tell her, does not stock navy beans or great northern beans or cannellini beans. No beans that look white. And adzuki beans, for what it's worth, are supposed to be a super food.

"They're so brown," she says.

That afternoon we find cannellini and borlotti beans in cans at City Super.

"Cans," I say. We can avoid cans at home. And do.

"I just don't like brown food."

Hong kind of watches me make the soup. Diced onion, peeled and diced carrot, diced celery, all sauteed in olive oil. While I'm about this knife work, I picture her beautifully cut carrots and celery in the first lunch she cooked and in every meal since then. I go about my chopping, feeling slightly ham-handed. I open three cans, pour beans and their broth over the sauté. Cans, I think. I'd bet anything Hong has never used anything from a can.

That night she sets the table, lays out the food she has prepared: handmade wontons with a vegetable filling, more broccoli and spinach, and another cabbage dish, this one with onion and ground pork that tastes, well, Chinese. My soup stays on the stove. I get it. We don't want Hong to think we don't like her food.

After Hong leaves that evening my daughter says to me, "I have to talk to Hong about meat."

We're launching the dishwasher Hong has loaded.

"The pork," I say.

"I think it was Fart Mart."

"Well." I happen to know it was from Fart Mart. I saw the package, the little yellow Styrofoam tray, the tennis-ball-size clumps of ground pork Hong formed, partitioned, wrapped, and froze for future reference. The cabbage we ate tonight, I figure, was a two-clump dish.

"It was packaged," I say. To its credit, FMart does have a meat counter. They don't allow the clientele to sink their hands into ground meats in the wet section of the store.

"Still," she says. "It's kind of gross."

IN 2015 CHINA REVISED its Food Safety Law. A Brookings publication refers to China's "food safety woes," adding, "China has done relatively better in enforcing food safety and quality standards for its food exports than it has for its domestic food market." Good news, I guess, if you live in Detroit; bad news if you live in Shanghai.

The revised law will require regions to establish "a standardized safe meat supermarket . . . to help stamp out tainted meat." Good! Each town and municipality will have a "demonstration store" to establish a food safety benchmark. According to *Global Meat* (I love the name of that publication) Fang Xin! will soon be the catchphrase for food safety, meaning "rest easy" or "be assured."

NO AMOUNT OF REASSURANCE will be enough for my daughter. It's City Super or bust.

The month we're here I'm in and out of FMart a number of

times. At first I'm put off by the noise. A guy is always posted mid-store with a microphone. He talks continuously in a tinny, amplified voice, calling customers to what's special today. Competing with him is another guy back in the wet section of the store. His delivery is not enhanced by technology. Lacking a microphone, he just shouts his invitations and blandishments. Obviously he was hired for his vocal cords.

Along with the noise FMart has an old-lady situation. Under other circumstances I love an old lady, the more the better, but these old ladies are aggressive. Tossing bean sprouts in a plastic bag, they look at you with a pitiless expression that says, *Get out of my way. You're going to die. I eat entrails.*

When the store is full, as at five in the afternoon, truckers continue to dolly food on pallets through the front door. The sea of shoppers parts. Evidently there is no back door, no storage space in the back of the store. The blue smocks stand and yack, arguing, laughing. At that time of day you don't walk the aisles in this store; you shove through them.

It's crazy, but if I lived here I would shop at FMart. Not for meat. Not for adzuki beans, if my wife had anything to say about it (which she would). But fruits and vegetables, yes. I can find the basics I need: onions, eggplant, cabbages, greens. And I would try to make sense of stuff I don't recognize: dragon fruit, Chinese green dates, oval white gourd, long sponge gourd, crown daisy chrysanthemum, winter bamboo shoots, iron yams, arrowhead. That's just a start. In bin after bin there are other fruits and vegetables and dried foods with no name in English, at least none that's printed.

In this strange, exotic country, for me the gateway would be FMart.

# 28

# The Fifteenth Floor

ONE MORNING WE WALK to the Montessori preschool our grandson attends. A few blocks from the school a man is lying on his stomach on the sidewalk. It's ten o'clock in the morning, a weekday in late January. The temperature is around forty-five degrees Fahrenheit. This man is shoeless and shirtless, both arms extended in front of him as though he's a swimmer diving into a pool. Under his left hand, visible between splayed fingers, is a small pile of banknotes. He's talking, maybe he's begging; to me it sounds like chanting or singing. Something tells me that even if I knew Chinese I might not understand what he's saying.

"Over there," our daughter tells us, pointing across the street. "The school is over there." She cups her hand around Gabriel's cheek, gently turning his head to redirect his glance, and steers us across the street.

In three weeks this is my only encounter with a street person in Shanghai, a city of twenty-four million people. Connie Maturana, writing for *Western Independent*, an Australian publication, observes, "It is during the quiet hours after midnight that Shanghai's homeless quietly begin to appear."

Which explains why I don't see them.

Another reason: the government takes care of them. *Manages* them might be a better term.

Rescue stations located around the city offer the homeless food, a bath, a place to sleep, provided they agree to be registered. Maturana writes, "Every homeless person now has their face photographed when they are registered into the station. For those that cannot be identified, their photograph is sent to the police database for identification. If within seven days no identification is made, a blood sample is collected and sent to police for DNA matching."

The government doesn't mess around. The preferred solution to the homeless situation is to ship homeless people back to their villages, which, it can be argued, is slightly more humane than what local governments in the U.S. do: buy them a bus ticket in San Francisco and ship them to Denver. In both cases, however, the goal is the same. Get them off the street.

I get the idea that homelessness is primarily a consequence of migration. China is in the midst of a massive migration of its rural population, moving people from their rural homes to urban highrises, mostly by fiat. In 1970 the population of Shanghai was 5.6 million; by 2020 the projected number is 27 million. In thirty years the urban population of China has increased by 440 million to about 660 million. (To get a feel for the magnitude of this mass of humanity, consider that according to recent census data the urban population of the U.S. is 245 million.) Some people, not surprisingly, slip through the cracks. To qualify for local services a Chinese migrant needs "hukou" status, which is local household registration. The government wants to know who you are and where you are.

We talk a lot about infrastructure in the U.S.: roads, bridges, airports, the power grid. China, it would seem, is good at all these things, and, despite the numbers, is also on top of keeping track of people.

You certainly see infrastructure here. There are cops everywhere, starting with the horn patrol, keeping the Shanghai streets quiet and civil. Then there's traffic patrol. All day long, on street corners and on the shoulders of roads, you see cops writing tickets (or more accurately, printing digital printouts that look like cash register receipts).

The main streets and sidewalks in this area are cleaned—swept, scrubbed, and rinsed—every couple days. On the way to coffee every morning I see a man picking up cigarette butts and small bits of paper with giant chopsticks. Within ten days of our arrival the road in front of this building was totally redone: resurfaced with lane lines painted yellow, bike and scooter and parking lines painted white. I never heard or saw a machine. The work literally happened overnight. Like the homeless the road workers must come out after midnight.

Which explains why I didn't see them.

Like most people in this city, our kids live in a high-rise apartment building. Their apartment is on the fifteenth floor. The near view: tile roofs of the French Concession buildings dating back to the nineteenth and early twentieth centuries. The far view: miles and miles of skyscrapers and high-rises, many of them brand-new. I say to my wife one day, "You don't hear much traffic noise." And it's true: the newly paved street, used by electric scooters, bicycles, and electric cars and trucks, monitored by the horn patrol, is very quiet. When our kids lived in lower Manhattan and we went to visit, traffic noise was constant and deafening. Then again, here we're on the fifteenth floor. The noise reduction may be engineered, but the noise is also way down below.

My wife says to me one day, "You don't see many kids." When we're out walking I've noticed that too. China has had a one-child policy since 1969. The results of one study I've scanned suggest the policy prevented four hundred million births (and created an aging population). Then again we're on the fifteenth floor. If you're on the street in front of this building at 11:15 a.m. or 3:30 p.m., when the school across the street lets them out, you see kids, many hundreds of them. So many you have to turn yourself sideways on the sidewalk to let them by. One day we visit the Shanghai Arts and Crafts Museum. We have the pleasure (really) of queuing up with hundreds of elementary school kids.

We're here for a month, helping our daughter with her children (one is three years old, the other four months) while she and her husband settle in. These four weeks we're sticking close to home. I walk the neighborhood every day. I like to think I'm getting a feel for local living. Again and again, on the other hand, I'm reminded of the folly of thinking we can understand much in such a short time. This is a difficult place.

The day we decide to go to the Long Museum to see a Rembrandt exhibit, it's raining hard. A good day to do something inside.

Like most of the corporate expats who live here, our kids have a driver. Wang takes my son-in-law to and from work; on crappy days (because of bad weather or dangerous air quality) he'll drive my daughter and the three-year-old to and from his preschool. If he's available he'll drive me and my wife around too. This day he is not available.

It's raining; otherwise we could walk.

"Take a cab," my daughter says.

That sounds easy enough. I look up the museum on my phone, photograph the name of the museum, written in Chinese, to show a cab driver. When I show my daughter she tells me to make sure we have the museum address in Chinese too.

"The driver might not know where the museum is," she says.

"I could say 'The Bund.'" Where the museum is, down by the river.

"He might not know what that means in English. They'll help you downstairs," she says. "Get the address."

When I ask James downstairs at the desk, he says he's never heard of the Long Museum. I show him the museum name, on my phone, written in Chinese. He shakes his head. He and the young woman working the desk have a lengthy conversation in Chinese, after which she does a computer search, takes out a post-it and writes on it, handing me the name of the museum, with its address, written in her beautiful script. Then she opens a drawer, takes out a card with the name and address of the high-rise where we live— written in Chinese.

Believe me, I've thought about this potential problem many times. If we venture far from home and get lost, how do we get back? Exactly *where* do we get back?

James calls the cab. Waits, and waits, and waits.

"It's raining," he says. "No cabs."

Right, like when it rains in Manhattan. No cabs.

We wait another five minutes, which I admit is pretty half-hearted, and decide to save this adventure for another day. We take the elevator back to the fifteenth floor. I feel kind of relieved.

Like most corporate expat families that live here, we can hire a nanny, an ayi. A few weeks after we get here Hong comes to work in the apartment. She's in her late forties. She's worked for a number of expat families, Spanish, French, Japanese. On the day we interview her and two other candidates, she's the only one who is comfortable holding the baby. We're all a little freaked out. This is new. There is no nanny history in our family. Still, our daughter will need help. Hong will look after the baby when our daughter walks the three-year-old to school on a good day, or rides with him on a bad-weather or bad-air day. Hong will cook, do laundry, buy groceries, be all-around helpful. She speaks a couple words of English.

The day she arrives Hong and I take my son-in-law's shirts to a cleaner. It's over by a soup place where my daughter and I have eaten. My job is to show Hong where to go.

On the way we stop at a fruit market. I pick up bananas and a bag of mandarin oranges. She takes the oranges from me and touches the skin on a few. She palpates a few more and shakes her head. Not good. She goes to the crate and picks up bag after bag, then sets them down. She turns and says something to the fruit vendor. A lengthy conversation ensues. The vendor finally gestures to a spot near the back of the store. Hong goes to that spot, bends down, and starts selecting oranges from a bin, one at a time. Finally she stands up and hands me a bagful, smiles, and nods. The vendor calculates a total. When I pull out too much money, Hong shakes her head. I'm pretty sure she rolls her eyes. She must think I'm a babe in the woods. At times I tend to think that too.

On the way there and back she walks a step behind me. She carries the laundry bag; then she carries the bag of fruit. When I offer to carry something, anything, she smiles and shakes her head. In front of a looming Bank of China we stand at a crosswalk, waiting for the green. When the light changes she hooks an arm through mine. There's no confusing it: this is a protective gesture on her part.

Hong knows things I want to know. I'd love to circle the block with her, stop at the fruit and vegetable stalls she likes, with the gorgeous fresh greens and baskets of eggs, past the hanging meats and fish baskets and the dried eels and ducks. Explain all this to me, Hong.

Back at the apartment, we sit down to the dinner Hong has prepared. Night falls quickly. Hong will ride forty minutes home on her electric scooter.

I stand at the window, gazing down, looking out at Shanghai, watching and listening for I don't know what.

# 29

# Chalant

"THAT GUY," I SAY to my niece, "has hair just like Tomy's."

We're standing in the Piazza del Popolo in Pesaro. It's the long midafternoon gap between lunchtime and the hour stores will reopen, a sunny day in November. A few women glide across the piazza on bicycles while this twenty-something guy strides past us, his black hair buzzed on the sides and back of his head, a shock of thick plumage sticking up on top.

"Half the guys his age in Pesaro look like that," she says with a laugh.

Black-frame glasses, a few days growth of beard, and the hair a thick hedge on top.

"Half the guys his age *in Italy* look like that," she adds.

Tomy is my wife's cousin's daughter's boyfriend. He has a shop that sells fresh pasta, cheeses, olive oil, truffle honey, chocolate spreads; assorted very good stuff. Before food he worked in men's fashion. While you talk to him in his shop he continuously looks past you and checks the windows in the front of the store, waving at fashionable people as they walk by. My niece is right. Half the guys he waves at look just like him.

"It's a young guy cut," I say.

"You weren't thinking about it, were you?" my niece asks.

"Not for a minute."

I've had a few haircuts in Italy. None of them have made me happy.

Some years ago I went to Simone, a guy who occasionally

cuts my wife's hair. My wife loves Simone. One year he's bald, another year he has kind of a butch cut. One year he has a goatee trimmed close to his face, another year he has scruff. When she goes into the shop he hugs her and kisses her cheeks, then he comes outside, shakes my hand, and kisses my cheeks. He asks, *Tutto bene?* "Everything okay?" Every year I am able to say two or three more things in Italian. *I like lunch! I drive a Fiat. Do you think it will rain?*

I didn't really need a cut that year. I wasn't in any immediate peril. I just thought, Why not? When you are an American in Italy you are perpetually conscious of the fashion edge they have on us. Especially in Pesaro, where it is not so much an edge as a precipice. I don't want to work as hard as they do at looking good; neither do I want to look conspicuously lazy or malevolently sloppy. That year I just sort of gave in. A haircut, I thought, could be mildly transformational.

The problem was twofold. How would I tell Simone what I wanted him to do? *Take a little off the ears, I'd prefer you didn't thin the back, I need enough hair in the front to tame my cowlick.* Haircut-speak is pretty nuanced. I asked my wife, "What's the word for cowlick?" *Ciuffo*, she said.

The second problem was not getting the cut everyone else wanted, the fashion cut.

That day, after we kissed, slapped shoulders, and established *tutto bene*, Simone got me into the chair. We looked at me in the mirror.

"Ciuffo," I said, pointing at the lock of hair above my right eye.

He smiled and nodded, obviously not yet sure what I wanted.

"No ciuffo," I said, to clarify. He gave me a searching look. He made a snipping gesture with the two fingers on his scissor hand. Did I want him cut the ciuffo off? I answered by making the same snipping gesture with my hand, then emphatically wagged an index finger, which means, in Italian, *Don't even think about it.* He said something very fast, little of which I understood. As I often do I shook my head in the affirmative and feigned understanding.

Next I grabbed the hair on the back of my head with both hands. "Non troppo magro," I said. *Not too thin.*

He started to laugh. He patted his stomach. He said he liked lunch too.

Wrong word for thin.

He moved around behind me and looked at my hair in the back, ruffled it a little bit. I began to think we had an understanding. "Facciamo cosi'," he said. *Here's what we'll do.* There followed a long explanation. I shook my head in the affirmative and feigned understanding.

"Okay," he said. In English!

I was outsourced briefly to a shampoo station, then delivered back to Simone's chair.

He cut. I watched. There was little barber banter, which was both kind of awkward and a relief. In a few minutes time I had used up my new Italian on him. *It's foggy. Last night I ate good cheese. I slept well.* He cut, and as I watched I began to think, *This is not going to be okay.* A lot of my hair kind of went flying. I put my best face forward. I nodded approval. What choice did I have? He cut, combed, sprayed some product on my head, brushed, and blew my hair to its logical, if unfortunate, conclusion. It was the default cut, the cut young guys had that year, thin in the back, thin above the ears, thin on top, and a sort of spear of hair in front, slanting diagonally across my forehead. Up there, above my right eye, he had liberated my cowlick.

"Okay?" he said.

My wife met me coming out of the shop.

"Oh, my," she said.

"I know," I said. The cut was transformational, not in a positive way.

For a few days every window I walked past, every mirror I looked in, was followed by that jolting moment of ir-recognition. Who is that guy? An imposter. Worse, a failed impersonation of an imposter.

NOT FAR FROM PESARO is the town of Urbino, where fifteenth-century humanist Baldassare Castiglione, in *The Book of the Courtier*, celebrated the concept of *sprezzatura*, which is translated as "studied nonchalance." In sprezzatura the individual demonstrates in attitude and action that he is "the total master of self, society's rules, and even physical laws . . . , unable to err."

On the street over the following days I was acutely aware of sprezzatura, of local people my age who looked better than I did, way better, without giving it a second thought. Late one afternoon my wife and I had *apperitivo* with my niece.

"It doesn't look that bad," my niece said.

I pointed at my forehead. QED.

"Do this," my wife said. She reached out and swept my hair to the left, then she swept it to the right. She started brushing at it, swatting it.

"Please stop."

"Didn't you tell Simone what to do?"

"In so many words."

A couple sitting at the table next to us leaned toward each other and spoke quietly. I imagined them saying, "What happened to that guy's hair?" The gentleman, maybe seventy years old, had short slate-gray hair, correctly cut, perfectly fitted to his head. He wore a snug light-blue sweater over a long-sleeved shirt, gray slacks, a scarf cinched around his neck. He was so well put together. He made it look so easy to wear those socks and those beautiful shoes. How did he do it?

In *The Rumpus* Lauren Cerand writes, "I have a theory that elegant people have an aura of impenetrable private sadness, and that good taste and impeccable manners are life's consolation." Well, maybe. On the other hand, that night, if anyone had reason to be sad . . .

The waiter brought them an evening espresso. They stirred sugar into their cups and sat reading the newspaper for a few more minutes. Then the couple got up and slowly left the bar, all fashion-able and correct, effortless and nonchalant.

A few minutes later the three of us followed them out.

I brought up the rear, temporarily looking like a walking error, totally and *irredeemably* chalant.

# 30

# Just Call

"ARE YOU GOING TO call the green number?"

My wife and I are in our rental car, a dark blue Fiat Panda. It's a four-door mini that feels like a grown-up go-cart. You can squeeze four small people and half a suitcase into it. It may be small but it's also brand-new. Its suspension is tight. It motors down the autostrada just fine at 120 kilometers per hour and squeaks into tight parking spaces in town. We don't need much in a car. This one exceeds our needs.

Except just now it's running on the spare tire. Earlier today, swooping in to parallel park the car in Pesaro, I got too close to the curb and ripped a three-inch slash in the right front tire. I'm sure the spare is safe, but it's also temporary. We'll be driving the car four more weeks. The car should have four good tires and a spare. What to do? Take matters into my own hands? Buy a new tire? And then return the car at the Bologna airport next month and pretend nothing happened?

"You really should call the green number," my wife says. "Find out what Europcar wants us to do."

The green number is toll-free help. I can make the call. I know I can make the call.

Still, it's the phone.

Over here I'll look a waiter in the eye and tell him exactly what I want to eat. I'll while away the time on the sidewalk in front of the apartment, talking to Luciana about her granddaughters. I'll blather away with the guy pumping my gas. Phone talk, on the other hand, makes me nervous.

I'm pretty sure Italian call centers, unlike those in the U.S., are not located in India. When I call I'm not required to decipher Italian spoken with an Indian accent. But that might as well be the case. There are regional differences in spoken Italian—variations in pronunciation and cadence—as well as buzzing phone connections and circumambient racket, as well as help desk staff that wake up in a bad mood or don't feel inspired by their work or get sick of talking to dopes like me who ask them, in half-assed Italian, to please repeat what they just said for the second, third, or fourth time.

I want to be independent, but I yield to the woman who speaks Italian.

My wife makes the call. In a minute she's got the answer.

"Don't buy a tire," she says. "Take the car to the airport in Rimini. Europcar will give you a different car."

"Good," I say. "That helps."

She sets down the phone. "I'm pretty sure he was Roman."

PHONE FEAR. MY MOTHER-IN-LAW, an Italian immigrant living in the U.S., was reluctant to answer the phone. (My father-in-law never answered it.) If she did, her response was brief and diversionary: *Hello? Please you talk my daughter, please?* When I was teaching, once or twice a year I got an Arab mom on the phone. I called looking for an Ahmed or a Hebah. "Hello," a woman I assumed was the mother would say, and I knew immediately she had little or no English. I could hear a definite vibration of fear in her voice. I learned to identify myself slowly. *Teacher. From the college.* This at least might keep her from hanging up. *Ahmed should call me,* I would say. Or *Hebah should come to class.* The call would end: *Yes* or *Okay,* sometimes just a nervous snicker.

In my initial trips to Italy I avoided the phone, pretty much the way I avoided driving. The time came when I wanted to drive and I needed to make calls, to restaurants, for example. I learned a little reservation lingo. I could tell the person on the other end of the line, "Reservation. Tonight at 7:30. Six people." Often in these calls I couldn't understand the greeting, which is a terrible way to start a conversation. Was I or was I not talking to Trattoria Marione? Or I didn't understand the response to my request. In Italy they say nineteen and a half rather than seven thirty, which assumes facility with both Italian numbers and European time conventions. (My numbers can be shaky. I recently told someone I came to Italy the first time in 1778.) Sometimes closing the call would rattle me. *A dopo*, I eventually gathered, means something like, "We'll see you a little later."

ON THE DRIVE DOWN to the Rimini airport I practice my explanation. I know the Italian verb "to park" and the word for "tire." Before leaving I looked up "curb" on Google Translate, but realize now that I've already forgotten it. At the airport I'll follow the sign for rental car return, which at other airports in Italy is always helpfully emblazoned in English. Inside the terminal I'll have to find the Europcar desk.

At the airport entrance there is no rental car return sign. In fact, the airport is almost totally deserted. A long, sweeping drive leads from the main road to the terminal doors, with room in front for half a dozen tour buses to park. There are no buses, no cars, and as far as I can tell no airplanes. Along the front of the terminal I see a series of automatic glass doors. At the far end, inside the terminal, standing in front of a coffee bar, is a group of men, twenty or so, a few of them in uniforms, cops or customs officers, I can't tell which. I park my Panda right next to the terminal and get out of the car. I would gesture *Okay to park here?* if someone looked. No one looks. The glass door in front of the bar won't open. The men drinking coffee either don't notice me standing there or they decide to ignore me. I fade down the front of the terminal, trying one door after another until finally one opens.

Inside I toy briefly with the idea of ordering an espresso, to establish my street cred, then think better of it. I tap a cop or customs officer, I can't tell which, on the shoulder and ask where the Europcar desk is.

"There's no Europcar here," he says.

"What about the lot?" I ask. "The Europcar lot?"

He shakes his head, points to the desert of empty pavement out front. As if to say: Do I seriously think there's a Europcar lot here?

I tell him my wife called the green number and was told to go to the Rimini airport.

"There's no Europcar here," he says again.

"They moved," a second guy says.

I ask where.

"Hey," the second guy yells, "anyone know where the Europcar lot is now?" He gets three or four answers, all speculative, all different. Another guy in a uniform gives me detailed driving directions, with five or six turns, to the Europcar lot. I understand turn right just before the gas station, I understand drive toward the sea. The rest gets blurry. I'm about to ask him to repeat what to do after the gas station when he says, "Wait, no, Europcar isn't there anymore."

"You'll have to call Europcar," the first uniformed guy says. He points on the car key I'm holding. "Just call the green number."

Just call.

I retreat from the bar, find the one door that opens, step outside, and climb back in the Panda. I take out my phone and open Google Translate, where I see: curb, *il cordone del marciapede.* Good grief. How long can I remember that?

A FRIEND OF MINE who travels a lot overseas advised me to buy a SIM card for my iPhone. While I'm in Italy, he said, I would have total continuity of service: email, browser, Facebook, Instagram, GPS, news updates, stocks, weather, SMS. And Translate. And, of course, when I needed it my device would also do its job, you know, as a *phone.*

He was right. I get out of bed in the morning and read the news. Just like at home.

Later in the day I wonder: When does the Coriano olive oil festival start?

I can check on that.

Walking around Bologna I wonder how many blocks we are from that wine shop on Via Malcontenti.

Let's find out.

My wife would like to send our kids a picture of the green ravioli we're having for lunch.

I'm on it.

Benefits galore. What I didn't anticipate was more interaction with Vodafone Lady, the friendly, informative automated voice of the phone service we use.

For the longest time I used a dumb phone in Italy. It was a primitive model, a pre-flip-phone phone the size of a Snickers bar. It had a cheesy ring I loved. To make the phone work I bought a Vodafone card at the local tobacco shop, phoned in the ten, twenty, or twenty-five euros to my account, had a brief (and always fraught) interaction with Vodafone Lady, and that was it. The phone was fine for the five or ten days we were here. I placed a call occasionally, the phone rang even less occasionally, and I answered and talked. Once or twice I had to call the Vodafone Lady to find out how many euros I had left. Or as she would say *il traffico disponibile*.

Now, with smartphone and a cellular internet modem, and a longer stay, I call Vodafone Lady more often. I drain the data plan on my phone. We run low on the modem data. I call to check on traffico disponibile. Vodafone Lady talks my ear off in Italian. It sounds to me like "standard Italian," not regional, that is. The problem is *how* she speaks: fast, very fast; in a burbling falsetto voice that must be a Vodafone committee's idealized version of your favorite Italian aunt. Listen carefully as she takes you through the ten options in the phone chain. If there were a feminine version of "avuncular," that would describe her. Nevertheless, when she talks I understand next to nothing.

"What's she saying?" I ask my wife one day.

She listens. "I don't know."

"But you're supposed to understand."

"That may be," she says. "But I don't. Why don't you go to the store?"

The Vodafone store? Those people are also hard to talk to. Take Vodafone Lady, give her two days growth of beard, a couple tattoos, and smoker's cough. Pick a number and wait. The service professionals are bored and grouchy. They probably wake up in a bad mood and don't feel inspired by their work and get sick of talking to dopes like me who ask them, in half-assed Italian, to please repeat what they just said for the second, third, or fourth time.

WHEN I CALL EUROPCAR from my Panda the guy on the other end of the green number speaks slowly and clearly. He gives me the address of the Europcar office, says it's near the train station. He says they will have a new car for me. I know where the train station is. To find the Europcar location I enter the address in the GPS on my iPhone and start driving. The iPhone lady directs me, speaking English, mispronouncing the Rimini street names. Her Italian pronunciation is more half-assed than mine.

At the Europcar desk the nice lady says she can't swap me into another Panda. Will a Twingo be okay?

Why not?

The Twingo is a little bigger than the Panda, brand-new, and will easily squeeze into tight parking spaces.

I've been driving the car a couple days when I realize it's missing the right rear hubcap. Did I do that? I could have done that. I'm sure I didn't.

"You should call the green number," my wife says.

How about I call the nice Europcar lady in Rimini?

Hubcap, Google Translate tells me, is *coprimozzo*.

On the phone the Rimini Europcar lady sounds a lot like Vodafone Lady. I tell her I'm the guy who traded the Panda for the Twingo. Yes! she says. She knows me. She sounds happy to hear from me. I can picture her behind the desk, and evidently she can picture me in front of the desk. This makes all the difference in the world. We are more than disembodied voices.

"Just a second, Mr. Richard," she says. "Let me check."

I hold the phone, waiting. In a minute she comes back on the line and tells me yes, the car was missing a coprimozzo.

"Tutto okay," she says. And if I have any questions, just call.

I will. I probably will.

# 31

# Say What?

WHEN YOU LEARN A foreign language it's difficult not to despair at first. How do you know which words you'll need? One of the first sentences I learned in French was a question. *Where is the library?* In hindsight I now know it would have been more practical to learn *Where is the bathroom?* A pal in high school learning German impressed me at lunch one day with a complete sentence in German. When I asked him what he said, he smiled and translated: *How many fingers has Anne?*

Much of my Italian I learned at the dinner table. Food Italian, it should come as no surprise, has come in very handy. Over the years I've branched out a little bit. I've learned to talk with some fluency about work, travel, and family. My limits, however, are always very much in evidence. The other day I told someone my parents died in the year 1215.

WHEN MY WIFE AND I are in Italy I'm not always fully *there*. Some days I'm more observer than participant. I listen but I do not always *hear*. Talk about limbo.

"I'm sorry, I don't understand what you said."

Usually that's my line.

One day my rental car starts saying that to *me*, in Italian.

"Mi displace, non ho capito cos'hai detto."

My wife and I have just pulled off the Autostrada. I'm delivering her to her favorite hair salon in Pesaro. At the toll booth I must have touched something somewhere in the car and turned on the Fiat lady.

My wife says, "What did you do?"

"Beats me."

"Mi displace, non ho capito cos'hai detto."

"I wasn't talking to you."

"What?"

"Fiat lady," I say. "I was talking to Fiat lady."

"Mi displace, non ho capito cos'hai detto."

"Maybe she thinks you want to make a phone call," my wife says.

She points at the little display window on the dash. It's mostly dark. Along the bottom there are writing and icons neither of us can decode. For one thing we're not wearing glasses. In addition, neither of us speaks Italian car. So far we've gotten along okay. The car beeps and chirps like a normal car to tell me stuff. A beep means *Fasten your seatbelt*. A chirp means either *Door open* or *Trunk not latched*. (It doesn't tell me which.) Along with these auditory reminders, on the driver's display are dinky little blue and red icons that I can't see without a magnifying glass. There's probably a trunk icon. I just can't see it. The other day I heard a long artificial tone when I pulled out of my parking spot. I couldn't get the car to go faster than walking speed. I floored it and we just ambled along. The tone—and there was probably an icon—told me why, a message, damn it, how was I supposed to understand? Finally I pulled over to the shoulder, shut the engine off, and restarted it. And away we went.

This is the first time the car has talked.

"Mi displace. Non ho capito cos'hai detto."

"Let's just go," my wife says. "I need to get to Marcello."

"I didn't say anything, Fiat lady."

"You've been talking nonstop."

"Not to her."

I reach for a radio knob and turn the volume down. In the

glove box is the Fiat manual. Read that later? I get a headache just thinking about it.

LATE THAT AFTERNOON WE walk up the street from our apartment to the local church. There's a memorial mass for my wife's departed uncle Giuseppe. In one of the little side chapels we join her old aunt, a few cousins, and a dozen people from town who enjoy a good six o'clock mass. My wife and I sit next to the old parish priest, Don Peppino. They whisper greetings to each other and visit for a minute or two, until a deacon walks in and takes a seat.

Ready? the old priest says.

The deacon nods. They launch into a rosary.

Wait, I thought this was a mass, I want to say to my wife. Thirty minutes and out. If it's a rosary *and* a mass we're in for a long slog. I've been to enough Italian funerals in the U.S. to know the rosary in English; in Italian I can pick out only a few key phrases: the fruit of your womb, the hour of our death, amen. For me the rosary in Italian is mostly an endless, droning verbal muddle. In the States I think they have both a short and long version. When I hear the word *mistero* I panic. We're doing long form.

At times like this I amuse myself by looking at people's shoes. It's an old crowd. On the ladies I see nice black flats, pumps, mules; on the men mostly shiny brogues and loafers. The deacon's brogues are impressive. They're scuffed, they've seen a lot of road, the lace ends on one shoe look frayed. The drone goes on. How many more joyful mysteries could there be? I've counted three so far. High along the near wall are stained-glass windows. Across from it the interior chapel wall has three shelves big enough to hold life-size statues. There's a friar, a Mary, and a Jesus holding a baby. No, probably Jesus is the baby, and Joseph, the invisible man with no lines in the drama, has made an appearance. The deacon sits on a folding chair beneath the Jesus shelf. The shelf is low enough, and the deacon is tall enough, that I'm worried he'll bang his head when he stands up. I picture him keeling over, falling unconscious to the floor, blood spurting from his head.

After the fifth mystery, more than enough mysteries for me, we wrap things up. The priest and deacon quit the room. The rest of us all sit in silence. No one moves.

"Is that it?" I whisper to my wife.

She shakes her head.

"Where'd they go?"

"The sacristy," she says, "to get ready for mass."

Huh?

"Robes," she whispers. And tells me to shush. They need different robes.

In the back of the chapel a nun dressed in a casual gray habit takes a seat in front of small electric keyboard, plugs the device in, and opens her music book. Just then the deacon and the priest come back in with a third priest.

I've been to enough Catholic masses back home to know it in English. In the States they make at least a half-assed effort to emphasize the bright side of things—alleluia, joy, resurrection. In Italian, judging by the tone of the language, it's totally different. It's all-out mournful. I sort of know what they're saying. Sin. Death. A woman gets up to read from the Old Testament. I get the text is Daniel; I make out furnace and Nebuchadnezzar (in Italian!). The third priest, prematurely old, officiates, consecrates, does his best to out-sad the deacon and old priest; the nun plays the organ, one dirge after another in which there's melody, sort of, but no chord changes. A whole hymn in the key of A? Really? Another one all in the key of F. And all so dreary. Basically everything sung in the key of death.

Near the end of mass, when the third priest's robes swish open, I see he's wearing bright green running shoes.

THAT NIGHT, MORE BABBLE. A first (for me, anyway): my wife and I go to a movie. It's called *Raffaello il Principe delle Arti*, about the painter Raphael. He's a big deal around here. Urbino, his birthplace, is just down the road. Supposedly the film is in 3D. Before we go, we can't figure out if the movie is drama or documentary. I'm really hoping for drama, with lots of straightforward, everyday dialogue.

The film is on big screens in all of Italy for only three days, which makes no sense to me. It must have something to do with cinematic supply and demand. We go, along with a cousin, to the last showing, starting at 9:30 p.m.

The screening room is downstairs. It's a large space with a low ceiling, reminding me of a church basement. Supply and demand indeed: when the lights go out the room is packed, and people are still arriving. I was seriously hoping to see a room full of Italians wearing 3D glasses, but the film we'll see, it turns out, is 2D, a ninety-minute documentary narrated by a nattily dressed art historian named Antonio Paolucci. There are no subtitles. (Why would there be? These people speak Italian.) Anyway we're sitting far enough back in the room, to please my wife, that I couldn't read them if there were.

Before I drift off to sleep I amuse myself by watching Italians in this setting. Shoes, of course. But also the extraordinary chaos of getting themselves all seated. It's Sisyphus revisited. Once the lights go out they continue to arrive and mill about in the aisles, iPhone flashlights switched on, talking talking talking. No one can find the right seat. No one is acquainted with the idea of assigned seats. (Row and seat numbers are indicated on the bottom of the ticket, in fine print, in *very* fine print. *Fila*: that means row.) For ten minutes, first in low light, then in the dark, a gentleman in a yellow sweater and fashionable red glasses leads his wife from fila to fila, looking for their seats. He, at least, seems to be enjoying himself.

After a lengthy visual prelude with copious explanation, most of which I do not understand, Antonio Paolucci comes on screen in full gesticulation, gushing about Piero della Francesca's painting *The Ideal City*. A few minutes later I open my eyes again and see Raphael's *Marriage of the Virgin*. Back on screen, Paolucci goes at it, explaining in a rapture of appreciation. He's way more fun to watch than the priest in the green shoes, but all the commentary, for me, remains a linguistic muddle.

At some point, between naps, I make out the word "la fornarina." Hey, you know that word. Wake up.

*Fornarina* is a thin pizza bianca served in some restaurants here just after you are seated. Think breadsticks, only flat, and just made. A fornarina is flaky with a sprinkle of olive oil. It emits an intoxicating fragrance of rosemary.

Also: La Fornarina is a restaurant in Urbino where we've eaten pasta with porcini mushrooms, pork roast, and field greens. Satisfactory house wine. Fourteenth-century room just below street level; arched ceiling. A very cool place.

Also: La fornarina is the name of a baker's daughter who served as the model for one of Raphael's most famous paintings, along with, I gather, quite a few Virgin Marys.

I open my eyes. There she is on screen, the baker's daughter, in a vignette dramatizing the meeting of the two. She is played by a comely young woman sitting at the edge of a mountain stream, bathing her feet in the water. Raphael, with that baby face and hair of his, approaches her. They exchange chaste glances. That's it. There's no dialogue. Any minute I know Paolucci is going to weigh in.

*Say something, you two,* I think. Like:

"I've had it with church. I'm skipping today."

"My uncle's wine is very good this year."

"I would like to paint you."

"This water is really cold."

No chat. The film shifts back to Paolucci, in a museum. Then we're in Rome, in the Sistine Chapel, in the Raphael rooms. I look, try to listen. But it's enough for one day. In a little while I'll be back in the Fiat. It will be a forty-minute drive home. I hope Fiat lady keeps quiet.

# 32

# Cowboys and Vespers

"WE COULD GO FOR vespers," my wife said.

It was late afternoon. We were leaving Murlo, which I have to say was something of a disappointment. Somewhere along the road in Tuscany we'd seen a billboard or two for Murlo, with its iconic cowboy image. And somewhere along the road in Tuscany we'd talked to someone, probably in a wine bar, who told us about it: Murlo, town of the Tuscan cowboys. It sounded like a football team.

When we got to Murlo there wasn't a cowboy in sight. There was barely anyone in sight. Evidently the Murlonians, I told my wife, like to keep to themselves. A British couple walking across the main piazza informed us that Murlo is famous for the inhabitants' DNA, which studies suggest is as close to Etruscan DNA as any in Italy. The Murlo cowboy icon, it turns out, is probably a representation of a *haruspex,* an ancient Etruscan dude who divined the future by poking at the entrails of a sacrificial goat.

No cowboys. No horses.

Not much fun.

"Well that was interesting," my wife said. "So how about we take in vespers?"

She really knows how to show a guy a good time.

"There's supposed to be a monastery nearby," she said. "It's called Abbazia di Monte Oliveto."

My wife loves a monastery. It takes her back to her Italian Catholic youth—processions, confessions, devotions, summer camp, fun with the nuns (she calls them *le suore*). At this monastery, with a little luck, we might hear some monks sing vespers.

I am partial to Gregorian chant.

"I'm in," I said.

This trip, I should point out, was pre-iPhone, pre-GPS. How to get there from Murlo? She took out the rental car agency road map, unfolded it, and laid it in her lap, looking for Buonconvento. No luck.

We were rolling out of Murlo when she pointed to an old guy by the side of the road. "Ask him," she said. "He looks local."

He did look local. Black coat, gray pants, hands joined behind his back. He was doing the old-guy walk.

I pulled off onto the shoulder and stopped.

Asking for directions in Italy can be frustrating. Often you are told to just keep going. "Sempre dritto," you'll be told. *Go straight. You'll eventually get there.*

The other possibility is a helpful person gives you detailed directions in the local dialect. That was the case with this old guy, who, for all I know, might have been speaking Etruscan.

IF YOU WATCH THE TV commercials today, you can be persuaded that technology offers a solution to problems like these. My favorite commercial features two people touring an Italian town. They've gone there to seek out ancestors. Finding an old guy like my friend standing by the side of road outside Murlo, one of them takes out his iPhone, holds it to his mouth, and says, "My grandfather came from this town. We're looking for his relatives. Do you know the Rossi family?" He then pecks at the translation app, which cobbles this message into grammatical Italian and pronounces it, in the audible voice of iPhone lady, to the old gentleman. In the TV commercial he nods, smiles, and says, *Hey! I'm your long lost relative!*

Well, maybe.

In reality, the old guy probably just says, "Eh?"

They jab the little speaker icon on the translation app again. iPhone lady repeats herself.

The old guy also repeats himself, only a little louder this time. "EHHH?"

The problem is her pronunciation.

Years later we're on the road again, this time looking for a restaurant called Kiosquito 46 in Riccione. I've Googled the address and invited iPhone to tell me how to get there. iPhone lady knows. She gives me directions in English. I understand her English. Her Italian not so much.

She says, "Merge onto Via Enrico Berlinguer."

Both my wife and I: "What was that?"

"At the next roundabout take the exit onto Viale G. de Verrazano."

"Onto what?" I ask my wife.

"I didn't get it. You have to take an exit."

"Can you ask her to tell you again?"

"I don't know how to do that."

I slow the car down. I'm hungry. Kiosquito 46 has great artichokes. What if we get there late and they run out of them?

My wife says, "Just keep going around."

"What?"

"Just keep circling the roundabout. She'll have to say it again. Maybe we'll get it."

iPhone lady repeats herself. We still don't get it.

"Turn the volume up."

"It's up all the way."

On the third lap we take the wrong turn and get rerouted. There are many more turns ahead of us. She gives us the scenic route. We listen intently as iPhone lady tries to say Via Casalecchio, Via Panzano, Via Piemonte, Via S. Lorenzo, Viale Giulio Cesare. It takes a while. We drive, stressed, a little bit lost, straining to understand. Eventually iPhone lady says, "Your destination is on your left."

Technology is supposed to help. A recent article in the *Guard-*

*ian* describes a new phenomenon called "death by GPS." A man in Yorkshire following GPS directions drives his car to the edge of a cliff. Somewhere in Australia a couple Japanese tourists, following GPS directions, drive their car into the ocean. "Satnav," as they call it in Britain, wreaks havoc on how we think when we drive. Studies show that "characteristic brain activity linked to simulating the different possible routes for a journey appears to be entirely absent when a person is following directions rather than independently planning a route."

Right. A few years ago a friend arrived at our house for dinner. When asked he said he had no idea how he got there. He had been delivered to us by GPS.

THAT YEAR WE FOUND Buonconvento and Abbazia di Monte Oliveta without GPS. It took us a while, but it was okay. We stopped and asked directions, then stopped and asked directions again. We just kept going. Eventually there was a sign, *Abbazia.* The drive around to the back of the monastery took us to a parking lot in a grove of pines.

"Peaceful," my wife said.

"Bucolic," I said.

"Shall we?"

I like the word "vespers." If evening prayers were called "crunchers" I probably would have been less cooperative.

We found the door to a chapel, took a stairway down to a stuffy room, and waited. It would be just us and the monks. After ten minutes or so, dressed in brown robes they filed in, ten or twelve of them, and sat. One of them set up an electric keyboard that reminded me, once he began to play, of the organ in Question Mark and the Mysterians' "96 Tears."

The monks got through their vespers. So did we. It was not Gregorian chant.

Out in the parking lot my wife said, "Well, at least we found it."

"Cowboys and vespers," I said. "Not a bad day."

It was getting dark. We had to find our way to a warm meal and a bed that night in Pienza, from a place that was not on the map. Years later we would have poked at the entrails of an electronic device.

That night I turned right at the main road, putting Murlo at our back. We went *sempre dritto*, believing that eventually we would see a sign.

# 33

# Planticide Now

THIS IS WHAT IT feels like to be a foreigner.

The people who live here, they see it in your clothes, in your walk, in the furtive movement of your eyes. As soon as you open your mouth you seal the deal. You're not from around here. At the grocery store the other day words failed me. I was in the cookie section. I'd walked up and down the aisle three or four times looking for a breakfast item. There was a guy who worked there, shoving boxes onto shelves. I stopped next to him and told him I was looking for... There came a long pause. In my Italian I said, *A type of*... He waited, fidgeted, I pantomimed spreading jam on a piece of bread, which didn't narrow things down much. In a panic what I thought was: I might starve to death before I remember this word. He gnawed his cheek for a few seconds, then started ripping open another box on the floor in front of him when, at last, I got it. *Crostini!* Sweets are in this aisle, he said. Breakfast stuff in the next.

A few minutes later, at the cash register up front, the woman who rang me up asked if I had something, it sounded like *sma*. It was a new word, kind of an ugly word. It sounded like a skin condition. I repeated it, putting a question mark after it. *Sma?* I said. *Thanks, I feel just fine.* The joke didn't land. Not even close. And why would it? She rang up the last of my items, scowled at my credit card, and slapped a receipt in front of me to sign.

The local word for us is *forestieri:* strangers; people from the woods.

The locals would do well to be suspicious. This trip I've come with a view to a kill.

When my father-in-law sold his stake in the family home to his brother over here, he walked a hundred meters down the street, probably that same day, strolled into a new condominium, and bought a two-bedroom apartment. It was 1966. Among the virtues of this apartment are the street-level front entrance, which means no stairs to climb when you come home laden with groceries, and a panoramic view of the mountain from the back of the apartment. In San Marino everyone wants a view of the mountain and the hilltop city with its three towers. You stare up into the face of something silent, awesome, eternal. When we arrive, the first thing we do is roll up the heavy serrande shutters, throw open a window, and, well, behold the mountain.

A few years ago we had my wife's friend Alba and her husband Fiorenzo over for dinner. I cooked, served; they talked.

"Let me get this straight," Alba said. "Your husband cooks?"

I set down dishes of pasta, penne in kind of a modified *arrabiata* sauce, with a little local sausage squeezed out of its casing, minced and cooked into the sauce.

Fiorenzo forked some, examined it. "Arrabiata should have *pancetta*."

Modified, I said. We had something like it in Tuscany.

Hmmm.

We ate. The three of them talked children, local politics and the rotten economy, the error of American foreign policy.

I brought out rabbit *alla cacciatore*, a few side dishes.

"Isn't he good?" my wife said.

Fiorenzo forked some, examined it. "We don't put olives in cacciatore around here."

Alba said, "Cut it out, Fiorenzo. It's good." She looked at me. "It's good."

Hmmm.

Fiorenzo gazed across the table and out the window. "You have a great view of the mountain in this apartment."

"It's one of the reasons Daddy bought it," my wife said.

"Yes," he says, "but you're going to have to cut down that tree." He called it a *pianta*, a plant.

Right, there is a tree.

It's a shaggy pine. Not a lot of branches. Picture a long-waisted scarecrow wearing a skirt. Right now its head and arms partially block our view of the three towers. In thirty years this tree has gone from a twig to five stories high. Its skirt gets higher and fuller every year. Down the hill below the tree is a road, a school; behind the school on the upward slope of the hill is a park and what they call a *pineta*, a full square mile of coniferous trees. It's designated by government as a no-build area, a green zone.

Add the pineta to the virtues of this place: all that permanent flourishing green behind us. Who would miss one tree? Would that be such a great loss?

So this year I contemplate an action. A hit.

My wife says one morning, "Let's go down by the sea today." We alternate. One day we walk up the mountain, another day we drive down to Rimini and walk down by the sea.

"Sure," I say. I've been looking out the window past the tree. If I lean out the window and bend hard to the right I can see two of the three towers.

"The tree," she says.

"Yes, the tree." It bothers her too. I know it does. "Nails might do it," I say.

"Do what?"

"I've heard you can kill a tree by hammering rusty nails into it."

"You're not going to do that."

"Every year we come, a couple more nails. Pretty soon it's an ex-tree."

Of course she says no. She loves a tree. Even a view-obstructing tree. And there's probably an ordinance.

Later, in the course of our walk down by the sea, I say, "What about salt?"

"What about salt?"

"Someone was telling me a good way to kill a tree is salt. You empty one of those big bags of salt, like for a water softener, around the base of the tree. Add water, wait a while, you get firewood."

"You would do that?"

It would have to be a covert operation. I could pull up next to the tree in the car in the dead of night, salt the tree. Circle back through town, come home and go to bed.

"And where are you going to get a bag of salt?" she says.

"I know a place."

"What, Obi?" Obi is Italy's Home Depot. They must have bags of salt.

After our walk we stop for coffee in the old part of Rimini. I have a few shirts I need to exchange. I really thought I was a medium. At home I cinched medium a while back. In the store a few days ago I tried on one of the shirts, buttoned it, stood there regarding myself in the mirror, front view, side view. It looked okay. It felt okay. I bought three. Back home I dressed in one of them for dinner. When I sat down the buttons pulled, and I suddenly felt ample and very full-waisted. A U.S. medium is a large over here, my niece tells me; small is a medium. So actually I bought a small. That's good to know.

Return means one of those encounters with an official person, a clunky explanation in my risky Italian. The young woman I present myself to in the front of the store is dressed in tight black. She has short brownish hair plastered back, with dabs of blue in the temples. I lay the shirts and my receipt on the counter.

"I made a mistake," I say. "Too tight." I turn sideways and foolishly trace the silhouette of my belly.

She tells me to go get the merchandise I want, bring it to her, they will exchange it.

I follow her directions. The transaction proceeds swimmingly until she asks if I want . . . something.

"What?"

She repeats the word, a little louder. Of course louder doesn't help. I still have no idea what she's saying.

Finally she says: "Do you want these?" She holds up the hangers.

"Attaccapanni?" I say.

"Gruccie."

"Attaccapanni."

"That's the other word," she says. "We say gruccie." I could see her thinking: *foreigners*.

"Done?" my wife says when I join her back at the coffee bar.

"Success."

I would have to work alone, go to Obi by myself. My wife will not be complicit in this act. *I'm looking for salt. A big bag of salt.* Maybe there's another word for that too. I begin to consider the weight of the bag, picture hauling it out of the trunk of the car, the pile of salt around the base of the tree. There may be a better way.

Back in the U.S., just before we left for Italy, my neighbor Therese was telling me about an earlier residence of theirs and a perfidious neighbor. She had a pool, this neighbor, and Therese had a tree, a gorgeous leafy maple. The leaves and the seed pods, basically any and all tree droppage, naturally found its way into the neighbor's pool.

"She was a terrible woman," Therese said.

I could sort of imagine.

"I went away one week," Therese said, "and when I came back the leaves on my tree were all pale and dropping. It was July. My tree was dying." She called a tree doctor, who examined the tree and pronounced it dead. "It can't be saved," the doc said. "You ask me, judging by the look of the base of the tree and its bark, this tree has been poisoned. Someone poured Roundup on it."

"Can you imagine?" she said. "What kind of a person kills a tree?"

She was devastated, of course. A tree is a thing of beauty. And the tree was there before the pool, long before. That should count for something. Just as the mountain, I think, was there long before our objectionable tree.

I would look in the Obi garden section. I would ask for Roundup (or whatever they call it) or something similar. What's the word for weed killer? for poison? It would take some explaining, some gesticulating, and probably that could be my undoing.

Suppose I were to succeed. I carry out the hit on the offending tree, it withers and dies, and someone not only notices and takes offense but takes *action*. The San Marino tree *dottore* or *dottoressa* comes, draws his or her inevitable conclusion. This tree has been *offed*. An investigator takes up the case, goes around and makes inquiries at places like Obi.

Have you sold a considerable quantity of Roundup (or whatever it's called) lately? Has there been anyone, you know, suspicious or *strange* in the store?

Well, now that you ask, there was a *forestiero* in here asking for Roundup (or whatever it is called). He talked kind of funny is why I remember.

How much did he buy?

Enough to wipe out half the green zone.

Can you describe him?

Short guy in his sixties, a little bit of a gut. He was wearing khakis and a shirt that was a size too large.

Must be an American.

They would get me in the end. I might be back in the U.S. already, safe, shielded from prosecution, unless there are extradition agreements between San Marino and the U.S. for crimes like planticide. They would get me, and I would have succeeded in becoming persona non grata, the *forestiero* who kills trees, making life difficult for all the other foreigners too, affirming the stereotype: sneaky, inscrutable, capable of skullduggery.

So I stay the execution, decide to make the best of things.

Sometimes you just have to tolerate the intolerable.

# 34

# The Cheese of Forgiveness

ASKED HOW I FEEL today, I'll say, "Fresh as a fish."

It's a figure of speech I heard on the TV yesterday, on a program that examined the quality and safety of fish from the Adriatic. We were at an inland trattoria eating *brassato*, a braised beef dish our friend Lidia makes. At noon, for the workers who come for lunch, Lidia turns on TV news. The focus was on fish. This was long-form journalism. Three journalists in a studio were importantly holding forth, along with reporters and scientists in the field hoisting octopi aloft by their tentacles, displaying crates of sole, mussels, and clams; a full half-hour exposé on fish. Given my limited fish vocabulary, I couldn't follow much of what they were saying. I recognized a few fish names; every so often I heard *inquinamenti*, the Italian word for pollutants.

When the program went to a commercial this phrase flashed on screen, in the interrogative mode: "Sano come un pesce?" I wondered about the quotation marks, thinking the phrase must be more than the title of the program. It had to be an expression.

"Sano come un pesce," I said to my wife.

"Healthy as a fish," she said.

"Is that something people say?" I asked her. "Healthy as a fish?"

"I don't know."

"Hello, how are you today? Fresh as a fish, thanks. How about you?"

"*Healthy* as a fish. I've never heard anyone say that."

"Fit as a fiddle. Fresh as a daisy. Why not fresh as a fish?"

She pointed to her plate and nodded at Lidia as she walked by. *Come burro*, she said. The meat was tender, like butter, they say in Italy.

I told my wife I was going to try out "fresh as a fish." Why not?

I've been collecting figures of speech. *Costa un occhio della testa.* High price. Expensive as an eye in your head. *Svelta come la polvera.* Describing a person. Fast as dust; agile, quick-witted. *Ogni morta di papa.* Something that happens infrequently, as often as a pope dies.

*Sano come un pesce.*

Then again, fish smell bad, even good fish. Maybe a person can't be fresh as a fish. Anyway I'm determined to try it out in conversation. *Come stai stamatina? Sano come un pesce.*

Next day we take to the road on what becomes a cheese hunt. We don't really choose this adventure. It finds us. We drive off in the direction of Morciano di Romagna. Every so often we pass blue road signs for hill towns —Gemmano, Montefiore, Saludecio, Mondaino, Montegridolfo—all within fifteen or twenty kilometers of each other. We're just above the Adriatic, on narrow roads winding around fields of grain, olive groves, and vineyards, rising to these old fortified towns. In Morciano, when I stop and ask some men in a coffee bar which town they recommend we visit, they confer gravely among themselves, puffing cigarettes and trading opinions in dialect, then say Montefiore, for the castle, or Mondaino, for the cheese.

We choose Montefiore, for the castle.

It turns out Montefiore also has a *santuario*.

In English a sanctuary can denote part of a church, a zone where wildlife congregates, or a hiding place for rebels and combatants. In Italy it's a holy place, where the divine is manifested, where holy people are buried, or where their relics (body parts such as fingers, throats, ears, noses, and hearts) are kept. My wife, a good Italian Catholic, loves a santuario.

We park in front of a coffee bar and *locanda* in the little piazza in Montefiore. When asked I inform the proprietor, Maurizio, that I am fresh as a fish today. He claps me on the shoulder and smiles. So it works. Or he tolerates foolishness. After coffee and rolls we tour the locanda: rooms upstairs (two with a fireplace he says with pride—and maybe we might be interested?), dining area, and cellars. When the castle was occupied, he tells us, in the fourteenth century and after, all the major properties in Montefiore were connected by tunnels. We go downstairs to see. Sure enough there's a tunnel. It's dark. He lights the way with his cell phone. There's a musty smell. And close, cold, damp air. Good for keeping the wine cool, he says.

"What about cheese?" I ask.

He wags a finger, no. "Too damp," he says. "In Mondaino, they burn straw in the pits to make them dry for the cheese. For the cheese, damp is bad." Mondaino, a few kilometers away, is famous for its *formaggio di fossa* (cheese from the pit), made from cow, sheep, or goat's milk, or some combination of the three. The cheeses are wrapped in bags and lowered into a pit that is sealed for eighty to a hundred days, allowing them to mature. On any menu in Romagna you are likely to find pasta served with formaggio di fossa. Its taste ranges from piquant to bitter to pungent.

"What do you think?" my wife says to me. "Castle? Santuario?"

"Or cheese," Maurizio says.

He hands us a brochure for Il Formaggio del Perdono (the cheese of forgiveness). The producer is Fattoria Sociale San Facondino, established in 1980 by a churchman named Don Oreste Benzi. Maurizio explains the program: The *fattoria* (farm) houses prisoners who are serving time. They live a wholesome farm life, learn cheese-making in the process, become, it is hoped, new men. On the brochure it says, *L'uomo non e' il suo errore*. Man is not defined by his mistakes.

"Santuario?" my wife says again.

My feet are hurting a little. I'm wearing new flipflops. We vacillate in English, tell Maurizio maybe we'll see the castle next time.

The santuario, he says, is just down the road. For the cheese of forgiveness we have to take the turn for Saludecio.

The road winds down the hill. It's green and shady and cool. As we approach the small religious complex, consisting of a church, a store, and crowds of pilgrims, we stop and start, mostly we stop and wait. The pilgrims are coming from all directions, men and women, young and old, in buses and cars, on scooters and bicycles, mostly on foot. I know my wife really wants to do this. I whisper, Do we really want to do this? We vacillate in silence. With no place to park and thoughts of lunch pressing upon us, we decide to seek the cheese instead.

Saludecio is easy. We follow the signs. When we reach the hill town the bells are ringing for eleven o'clock mass. We stop and talk to someone walking past the church. (I wait for the right moment to announce I am fresh as a fish. It never quite presents itself.) When we are joined by a few more passersby we ask about the cheese of forgiveness. Everyone seems to know about it. Drive down the hill, we are told, toward Cattolica (yes, a town called Catholic). Along the way we'll see a church and a fork in the road. Go right. The farm is down there.

I ask, along the way roughly *how far*?

Not too far. We can't miss it. Follow the signs for Cattolica. Look for the church and the fork.

It sounds easy enough, except there are a few churches at intersections, and some of the intersections look vaguely forklike. Ten minutes or so down the road, when I'm beginning to think we've missed it, there's a church. And a fork. My wife has a feeling, says jog to the right.

"You think this is the turn?" I ask. The road is paved, lane-and-a-half, small-car Italian size. We're the only car, pointed in the direction of the middle of nowhere. It's a very pleasant nowhere, but still nowhere. There is no pilgrimage to the cheese farm today.

"There was a church," my wife says. "This must be it."

I slow the car, move to the edge of the road. "Was there a sign?"

"I didn't see a sign."

"Shouldn't there be a sign? Cheese of forgiveness, this way?"

"Everyone knows about it. Maybe they don't need a sign. Maybe you can google it on your phone?"

I pull into a paved parking lot and google around, fighting autocorrect, and find nothing. "Zip," I say. "Un bel niente." A beautiful nothing.

She points. A kilometer or so down the road the aluminum roofs of a couple barns reflect the bright sunlight. "Let's go down there."

"A halo," I say.

It's a farm, all right. Lots of hay. No people. No cheese.

We drive back and forth, trying not to lose heart, return to the road to Cattolica, where we find a woman walking along the shoulder who of course knows all about the cheese of forgiveness. We talk for a few minutes. I'd like to tell her I'm fresh as a fish, but again the moment isn't right. Yes, she says, we took the right road. We just have to continue down that road for a while, beyond the hay, until we see the cheese place on the right.

I ask, How far beyond the hay?

Not too far. She says we can't miss it.

We execute a U-turn and go back to the church and the fork. "Do we really want to do this?" I ask my wife.

"We've come this far."

"It's seems like a lot of fuss for some cheese."

"It's an adventure," she says. "What if it's right there? Shouldn't we at least try?"

It turns out we *were* almost there. Not far beyond the hay there is a sign on the right by the side of the road, small black letters painted by hand on a white board the size of a pizza box, *formaggio*, and one lane of dirt road so rough I have to drive at walking speed up a hill, over a crest, and down the hill, past a couple houses, winding down a kilometer or so into a valley until we reach a structure too big to be just a house, with a long drive and, in the back, in front of a white facility that has dairy and cheese written all over it, a tractor and a young man standing next to it.

His name is Giovanni. He looks thirty or so. He is wearing jeans and has tattoos up and down both arms. He says he's from Florence. He says he never imagined living in the country like this, taking care of animals, and making cheese. He takes us inside the facility. We walk from cooler to cooler, where there are racks of cheese from floor to ceiling. He has fresh *caciotta*, caciotta with nuts, caciotta with pepperoncino, mozzarella, ricotta, and *scamorza*. We ask to try the fresh caciotta.

He unwraps a wheel and cuts two slices with a long knife.

"Do you eat the rind?" he asks. "It's okay to eat the rind. But not everyone likes it."

We eat our slices, rind and all, and buy two wheels of Giovanni's fresh caciotta, along with a small tub of fresh ricotta.

We chat for a few minutes about who we are and how we found the cheese of forgiveness. Giovanni is knowledgeable, happy we are interested, pleased to talk about cheese. He shows us how to scrub the cheese if the rind starts to turn green, which he guarantees it will. If the rind changes color, he says, don't worry. The cheese is still good.

"You just run cold water over it," he says, "and scrub it clean with a brush."

He finds a wheel with a coat of green, goes to a sink, and washes it. "See?" he says. He holds it up. It's clean and white. "It's that easy."

Clean cheese. It's a special moment, both for him and for us. We thank him and take our cheese and slowly drive back up the hill, back to the main road, feeling good, feeling fresh as fish, maybe even better.

# 35

# Please, After You

CARS ARE LINED UP behind me.

I'm at the Pesaro toll booth on the A-14. Usually there are at least two booths open, one automated, one manned by a late-middle-aged guy in a light blue shirt. Typically he's smoking. Typically he has great hair and snazzy glasses. Typically he's talking to one of his associates while your transaction takes place. The toll display blinks the amount you owe. You pay and you go.

Even when I have exact change I usually take the booth with the guy. In the automated line every idiot in front of you has to figure out how to insert his ticket. Then he has to dig change out of his pocket, count it, and figure out where to put money in the machine. Inside the mechanism the coins spin, slide down a chute, and drop, finally passing through the automated counter. There's a long, long wait until the gate opens and an automated female voice says, *Arrivederci!* Or, horrors, the money is short and she asks for the rest of the toll, in which case the above process repeats itself.

Today there's only an automated booth.

And today I'm the idiot.

The toll is 2.30 euro. All I have is a five. When I insert the bill the machine spits it out. *Please do something*, the automated female voice says. I have no idea what she said. I turn the bill over and try again. Ejected again. *Please do something.* Still didn't get that. Behind me a horn honks my idiot status. On the machine I look for something to tap, a button to push, anything. *Please do some-*

*thing. Please do it now.* I keep turning the bill over, inserting it. Another honk. And then another.

Once, twice, three times an idiot.

Through the speaker on the machine, a blue shirt says *something*. I tell him I can't insert my money into the machine. He says *something* again. Behind me all the horns wonder if I heard them. Just then blue shirt is standing between my car and the machine.

"It won't take my bill," I say.

He casts a weary glance at the cars lined up behind me, takes my money. He tells me sometimes the machines have a mind of their own.

Seven or eight cars backed up. Everyone molto agitated.

The line is a special form of hell everywhere, but Italians seem to have a special antipathy for them. Writing for *La Repubblica*, Francesco Piccolo observes, "Your life is conceived with one purpose in mind: Do whatever possible to avoid lines." When you stop at a traffic light, teenagers and adults on scooters zip around and between cars to get to the front of the line. In church, at the call to holy communion, it's a total mob of believers from all corners of the church, pressing to the center aisle, urging forward toward the altar. It's not, *What if they run out of Christ before I get there?* It's not, *I'm in a hurry because I have a chicken in the oven at home.* It's just what they do. At Amsterdam airport I watched an Italian nun cut the line at passport control. She cut it again when we boarded our flight to Bologna.

Some years ago a friend of ours was in line for tickets at the train station in Rimini. She waited in line, American style, while one Italian after another pushed in front of her or executed lateral entry and bought their tickets. When she got to the ticket window our friend said to the blue shirt, "Excuse me, why do you let people cut the line like that?"

He said, "Signora, my job is to sell tickets. If you're going to let people cut in front of you, that's your problem."

It's a strain of anarchy in the Italian character, greater than or equal to the American respect for the line.

One year my wife and kids and I were in line at Greenfield Village, an outdoor museum in the Detroit area. The kids were small. It was Halloween night. We had to get to the front of a long line for something, to get a trinket of some sort, I think.

"Come on," my wife said.

"What?"

"We're cutting the line."

Our daughter, seven or so, already indoctrinated by a few years of schooling to respect the line, looked up at her mother, mortified.

"Really?" I said, shifting our son in my arms. He was heavy. It was cold. "Really, we shouldn't."

"Come on."

So we walked, sidled, sort of meandered our way forward. The lane was lined with pumpkins. Johnny Appleseeds and Walt Whitmans and Goodie Proctors greeted us as we walked. Ten feet or so from the front of the line we gently merged. In a few more minutes it was our turn. The kids loved their trinkets.

"I can't believe you did that," I said to my wife.

"Get over it," she said.

It's taken a while. I'm starting to get over it.

You detect aggressive piety about the line on roads in the U.S. You're southbound on I-275. In two miles, signs indicate, the left lane will close for road work. Well ahead of the closure some drivers ease to the right, slow down, maybe even stop, leaving the left lane wide open for a mile or more. So you are faced with a dilemma: proceed as far as possible as fast as possible in what remains of the left lane, or move right, slow down, maybe even stop. Usually it's a pickup truck or a big very car; usually it's an older white guy. He's crawling along in the right lane, boiling with righteous indignation because of the a-holes who are flying by him in the one mile or so of the not-yet-closed left lane. So he fades slightly left, holding his place in the right lane, blocking the left lane, deciding, in effect, to close that lane early. I'm sure he's a freedom-loving fellow. He simply takes it upon himself to limit your freedom to access the mile or so of the not-yet-closed left lane. To him you're cutting the line. It's undemocratic. To me it's a gray area. Anymore, usually if it's gray, I go.

One year I was flying home from Rome. It was late June. It was hot and humid. Little or no AC in the terminal. Nerves can get raw. Alitalia check-in was open, but the line was long, very long, and the flight was a little bit delayed. People in line slumped on heaps of luggage, skidding bags forward a few inches at a time. I was slumped with them, many of them my compatriots. Every so often a bunch of Italians arrived, in their sunglasses and sweaters and jackets and scarves, long-legged thin guys in red slacks and yellow slacks and nice shoes, women in leather boots and tights and ropes of shiny necklaces loosely draped around their necks, striding confidently, all of them, to the front of the line, probably to make inquiries is all, probably turned away by the blue shirts working for the airline way, way up there at the front of the line.

Well look at them, I thought. And waited.

A few piles of suitcases in front of me was an American guy who watched this traffic, unnerved.

"What are they doing?" he said to his wife.

She fanned herself and shook her head.

"What do they think they're doing?" he said.

Five or ten minutes passed. Eventually he couldn't take it anymore. As soon as he saw the next group coming he stood athwart the lane and said, "You'll have to go back." Waving his arms at them in case they didn't know where the back was. "The end of the line is back there," he said. "You have to go to the end of the line."

Palm up, the baffled Italian brings his thumb and first three fingertips together, then gives his hand a gentle shake in someone's general direction. In Italy this means, *Have you totally lost your mind?*

It was not a gesture that engendered great friendship between nations, any more than the waving arms did.

A few nights ago my wife and I were in a small piazza down in Rimini for *aperitivo*. It's a convivial late-afternoon, early-evening ritual lasting two or three hours. You sit outside under umbrellas and have drinks and snacks. You watch people come and go. This place we've adopted is called La Bottega. The service is fast, the snacks are good. Every night La Bottega is packed. There's lots of local color. An added attraction: on the sound system, best heard indoors, they often play American music of the fifties, sixties, seventies. Go inside for food, enjoy a little music. I was filling my little plate this night with ceci beans and mortadella finger sandwiches when Johnny Cash came on the system. That deep, soulful, singular country voice of his: "Because you're mine, I walk the line."

"Che bella voce," someone said.

Ceci beans and Johnny Cash. It was like having instantaneous contact with both cultures.

Five or six of us breasted the buffet, eyeing the trays. They were running low on the sandwiches. One after another we yielded to each other. *After you. Please, after you.*

Courtesy can break out when you least expect it, even when you're standing in line, and isn't that nice.

# 36

# When Bacco Smiles

MY WIFE'S OLD AUNT has an *omino* (the diminutive of *uomo*, the Italian word for "man"). Omino. Little man. When she wants to cook a rabbit for lunch she has an omino who sells her the rabbit. She wants fish, she has another omino. She has a repair job to do in the house, she calls a different little man. We were having lunch the other day, a baked *orata* she got from her fish omino. I asked her about the wine. Dark red, slightly frizzante, in a full-liter bottle with a metal cap, no label. She says—of course—she has an omino.

"He lives just over there." She points a crooked finger toward a hillside. "He's been bringing us wine for years."

I want an omino.

In particular I want a wine omino.

One of the special pleasures of being in Italy is local wine. It's young, it's light in alcohol content, it's great with food. And, by American standards, it's incredibly cheap.

Consider the carafe—that ubiquitous vessel gracing the trattoria table. There are days we order a quarter liter, or a half liter, or sitting down to eat with a large appetite and the prospect of many luxurious foods, we know we're going to need a full liter. All the years I brought people to Italy on eating excursions, they inevitably extolled the virtues of the wine. They would say, What is it about these Italian wines? I don't get tipsy. And no headache. I can't get enough of it.

For some time now, when I buy wine I go to Zonzini. It's a

store just down the road from our apartment in San Marino. He is part wholesaler, part retailer, a purveyor of, among other things, bottled water by the case, chocolates, liquor, and wine. The high ceiling and cement floor, along with the floor-to-ceiling metal racks, give the place the feel of a warehouse. Behind the cash register there's a stock of wines from all over Italy. You can go back there and look. Typically I stand in front of local wines, the ones from Romagna, and I select Sangiovese Superiore. My criteria for selection are attractive label and price. The wines come from nearby towns, Imola, Predappio, Cesena, Bertinoro, San Patrignano. Until recently I had my standards. I would not go lower than five euros for a bottle.

That was then.

Alas, Bacco has smiled upon me.

I have an omino. Her name is Francesca.

Okay, so she's not a little man. And technically she's not really an omino because she works in a store. Your standard issue omino does not have a website; he has a farm. But I'll take her.

Across from the *mercato centrale* down in Rimini, a sprawling fish-meat-vegetable-fruit market, I notice this store one day: I Vini delle terre di Malatesta. It's well lit. It looks like a high-end *enoteca*. Lots of racks, lots of bottles with attractive labels. Except that in the back corner I notice two faux kegs protruding from the walls. On each keg two spigots. Three reds, one white. For each wine there is information about its source, alcohol content, and price. This store sells *vino sfuso*, the stuff you get in trattorie by the carafe.

"Bring your own bottles to the store," Francesca explains, "or we have bottles you can buy, and fill, and reuse. Buy as much as you want."

I taste two reds, a Cabernet and a Sangiovese, and choose the latter. She fills a handsome bottle, packs it in a thick take-it-with-you sack. All for three euro. In the U.S. the sack alone would cost that much. I take the wine home and love it.

IN FIFTY YEARS ITALIAN wines have come a long way. In the American consumer's view, such as it was, Italian wine was kind of a joke. Buy a straw-covered Chianti fiasco, pour out the wine, and plug up the bottle with a candle. It was like Mateus. Great bottle. The wine? Meh. Then again, fifty years ago Americans were not wine drinkers. And the Italians were smart, my wife likes to say. They kept the good wines for themselves. No doubt that's part of the story. So many omini, so much good local wine.

Then along comes Giovanni Mariani Jr., son of Giovanni Mariani Sr. The latter founded the House of Banfi in Greenwich Village in 1919. Mariani the younger introduced Lambrusco to the American consumer in 1969, sold twenty thousand cases of the stuff that year, then fifty thousand cases the next year. By 1975 imports of the bubbly sweet red had increased to 1.2 million cases, by 1984 to a whopping 11.2 million cases. Lambrusco is a wine you drink cold, a forerunner of that unfortunate American contribution to wine culture, the wine cooler. (I remember a night out in Columbus, Ohio, in the midseventies with a couple friends, cruising bluegrass bars, guzzling Black Russians, and finishing the night drinking Riunite on the rocks.) Riunite and Cella wines established the Italian footprint, or wine stain, in the American market. According to Funding Universe, "By 1980 Banfi alone was bringing more wine into the U.S. from Italy—some nine million cases a year—than France and Germany combined."

Thanks for that sweet red wine, Banfi, we might say. The wine was pretty bad. But there's more to the story. One word:
Brunello.

In 1977 the Banfi organization charged oenologist Ezio Rivella with finding the perfect location in Italy for a vineyard. He was their omino. He did his job. The place he found was Montalcino.

Today a Brunello di Montalcino will sell for up to $250 a bottle. American wineheads flock to that far-flung Tuscan town. Rory Carroll, writing for the *Guardian*, reports, "Those who get to taste [Brunello] come away drooling adjectives such as intense, full-bodied, fruity, smooth, rich, chewy, velvety, super-ripe, spicy, gigantic. In the battle with the new world, Montalcino stands as a citadel of old world might and venerability."

And today Coldiretti, an Italian grower-producer organization, boasts that Italy is the largest wine exporter in the world. In 2013 the U.S. imported $1.3 billion in Italian wines.

In omini we trust.

PROBABLY EVERY TRATTORIA AND osteria in Italy has an omino. He's the proprietor's cousin or uncle, he's a farmer with some vines who makes local swill that's dirt cheap and consistently good. The omino's *vino sfuso* graces the table, complements the food, goes down easy.

Except when it doesn't.

In Novilara, in the hills above the Adriatic, is a restaurant where we eat *tagliatelle* and beans. The food is something of a religious experience; the house wine, on the other hand, for two of three consecutive years was terrible. It was kind of a joke. But not.

And just last week my wife and I had lunch in a Pesaro trattoria. At the table next to us a couple local guys ordered wine by the glass. The server did not stand on ceremony. He didn't show the label or smell the cork or linger and watch as the guys swirled, sniffed, and sipped. This was a joint. He brought them stem glasses, the wine already poured, then he brought them their food. I confess at the moment I felt just a little smug. We ordered the house wine. Don't they know how good it is, how simple and delicious in bistro glasses? When the server came to our table and set down a half-liter carafe of red I turned over my bistro glass, poured some wine, and had a taste. Someone's uncle must have had a very bad year.

Then there's Fabio, our new friend. A couple nights ago we had dinner at a local *agriturismo* that serves *strozzopreti* with *sangiovese*, sausage, and radicchio, a dish of pasta that is life changing. And the wine was exceptional.

"It's a sangiovese," Fabio said, "with a little merlot added. You can taste the merlot—it makes the wine a little rounder."

I wasn't really sure I knew what round tasted like, but I nodded my head.

He said this year the grape harvest was not very good. They didn't make wine.

"If you don't have good grapes," he said, "you can't make good wine."

They still had a lot of wine from the year before, enough to get them through the year. We could buy some if we wanted to; a bottle, a five-liter jug, as much as we wanted.

In omini we trust.

Trust, yes. But verify.

# 37

# Have I Got a Ragu for You

I WAS READING THE other day in *The Daily Beast* about Mario Batali's friendship with Jim Harrison and their "search for the genuine." Harrison's final book, *A Really Big Lunch*, a posthumous collection of his madman essays on food and drink, was about to be published.

My mind turned to a favorite subject and my search for the genuine.

Ragu.

You might say I have been immersed in ragu for decades, since marrying a woman from the Republic of San Marino, which is roughly an hour's drive from Bologna. Bologna and surrounding towns in Emilia-Romagna are the rich beating heart of ragu country in Italy. After joining the family, over the years I learned to love her mother's ragu; then, after he retired and approached the stove, her father's ragu; then, at her relatives' trattoria in Spadarolo at the edge of Rimini, her cousin Marco's ragu. Eventually, having eaten around San Marino and the valley of the Marecchia for a number of years, I fashioned my own approach to that staple of the Romagna table.

So I was eager one night to have Alberto Alberti over for dinner. He was one of my wife's work associates, an Italian temporarily in the U.S., from Cento, just north of Bologna. Pasta in American restaurants is almost always a disappointment—overcooked, mushy, and wet. I imagined him wandering the local foodscape looking for a decent dish of pasta. That night I thought we would present Alberto with something close to home, a dish of *tagliatelle al ragu*. Let your search for the genuine in the Detroit area end, I could tell him, here at our table.

He brought a bottle of Lambrusco, red wine from his part of the country. I stifled my urge to comment: *Yick*. (Unfairly or not, I will always associate Lambrusco with swill imported from Italy in the early seventies, immortalized in a slick ad campaign featuring an Italian dandy named Aldo who, surrounded by adoring women, ended every commercial burbling the ad's tagline: *Chill a Cella!*) For fifteen minutes or so we sipped the slightly sweet, slightly *frizzante*, slightly chilled wine and rolled slices of prosciutto and mortadella onto breadsticks. When at last I brought the platter of pasta from the stove Alberto Alberti looked startled.

He pushed back from the table. "What's this?"

"Tagliatelle," I said.

He shook his head and waggled a finger over the dish. "I mean this . . . sauce."

"Ragu," I said.

He shook his head and announced that he couldn't eat it.

Years of apprenticeship at Romagnolo tables, both here and abroad, had gone into the making of that ragu. I was surprised, flummoxed. A little bit pissed.

"I don't like tomato," he explained. He added, to my horror, that what I had cooked wasn't really ragu.

"Of course it is," I said.

Well, he said, whatever. It wasn't *real* ragu.

REAL RAGU. IS THERE such a thing?

Ragu, from *ragout*, from the French *ragouter,* meaning "to revive the taste of," has graced European tables for hundreds of years. Until recently, especially in the English-speaking world, it was a dish in search of respect.

Where ragout is concerned, if there was a recurring theme it was anything goes. In Francatelli's *The Modern Cook,* first published in 1846 at the University of Leeds, along with a common vegetable base tasty ragouts feature a variety of animal proteins: roe of mackerel, lobster, crayfish, eel, chicken wings; and by today's standards some oddities as well, such as cockscombs, larks, ox palate, calf's head, sheep's tongue, and sheep's feet. *The Compleat Housewife*, an eighteenth-century compendium of good culinary practice, includes recipes for ragouts of pig's ears and lamb testicles.

As a college student I recall encountering the term "ragout," perhaps for the first time, in Jonathan Swift's essay "A Modest Proposal," a satirical take on the problem of poverty and hunger in seventeenth-century Ireland. Oddities indeed. Swift muses, "A young healthy Child well Nursed is at a year Old a most delicious, nourishing, and wholesome Food whether Stewed, Roasted, Baked, or Boyled, and I make no doubt that it will equally serve in a Fricasie, or *Ragout*" (my emphasis). (Of course Swift wasn't really saying eat the children of the poor; he was saying for the love of God feed them, and feed the rest of the poor, too, while you're at it.)

Another recurring theme: stews and ragouts were foreign, a confusion foisted upon the proper English eating population, a "kickshaw" (from the French *quelque chose*). In *The Memoirs of a Femme de Chambre* (1846) the narrator observes, "I feel quite uncomfortable having eaten many kickshaws . . . [G]ive me a joint of well boiled, or roasted meat, in preference to all the French stews and ragouts in the world, which clog, without satisfying the stomach." In the writing of Lord Shaftesbury, a contemporary of Swift, it becomes clear that ragouts and stews are frowned upon. Here, for example, Shaftesbury laments the diner's "inability to distinguish between different ingredients—vegetable and animal look alike, and the different parts of animals' bodies, once dismembered and submerged in sauce, are indistinguishable as well."

Both Swift and Shaftesbury would have been acquainted with the writing of Juvenal, the Roman satirist who turned up his nose at stew. According to Emily Gowers in *The Loaded Table: Representations of Food in Roman Literature*, "Juvenal charts the precipitous descent of a gourmet from his world-wide search for dainties to the mixed scraps of the gladiators' school," pointing to "the wretched mixed dishes in the bowels of the Roman Empire."

Many ragouts: basic grub.

Ragout arrived in Italy near the end of the eighteenth century, probably thanks to Napoleon, and the Italians did what they do: take something good and make it better.

They made ragu.

According to the historical record classical ragu, Alberto's real ragu, was born in the late eighteenth century in Imola, a fortified city in Emilia Romagna, southeast of Bologna. This ragu was the brainchild (or food child) of one Alberto Alvisi, who cooked for Cardinal Gregorio Chiaramonti, the future Pope Pio VII. The recipe calls for salt pork; chicken, beef, or pork; onion, butter, chicken stock, and flour. And ground cinnamon. It was made to be served with *maccheroni*, the generic term for pasta at the time. A cardinal ate it, so you know this was not a dish for poor people. Lynne Rossetto Kaspar, author and voice of *The Splendid Table*, reports that through the nineteenth century, until and even after the unification of Italy, pasta with this meaty ragu remained a dish for the wealthy classes due to the cost of meat and pasta.

Alvisi's recipe is the antecedent of what we call Bolognese sauce today. His recipe is notable for what it lacks—tomato. A great deal of ink and angst has been spent in Italy on the proper place of tomato in ragu—in the pot or not. In all likelihood tomato was added to the recipe because meat was expensive. Tomato "lengthened" the sauce, thus becoming the ragu as we know it today, or a facsimile of it.

In Italy, all over the real ragu region, I've had it with tomato and without. More commonly with.

MY FIRST ENCOUNTER WITH RAGU, known more widely back then by the term "spaghetti sauce," occurred when I was a kid. The rage when I was in high school was pizza in a box. Not the flat, square takeout boxes we know today, made to fit pizzas of various sizes, ranging from Frisbee size to LP-vinyl-disk size to garbage-can-lid size. Pizza delivery had not yet reached the one-stoplight farm town where I grew up. There was a takeout joint in Saginaw, eight miles down the road, called Luigi's. It might as well have been on the other side of the ocean.

No, this was a Chef Boyardee make-your-pizza-at-home pizza. Inside the box was a plastic bag of dough mix you added water to, another plastic bag containing a rancid-smelling mix of pseudo mozzarella and parmesan cheese, and a small can of tomato sauce. The sauce was red, runny, and pungent, with bits of tomato-esque matter and oregano floating in it. Of course we used all of it. Some-one smarter and more worldly than we were had determined how much sauce a pizza needed. *Lotsa.* When we poured it over the dough we had mixed, massaged, and squashed onto a cookie sheet, when the sauce fumes reached our nostrils, we felt a vague connec-tion to something exotic. The results were tragic: a lumpy, gooey pizza only clueless high school kids could love.

The stuff in that can, call it pizza sauce, spaghetti sauce, or ragu, held sway for years in the American market.

RAGU HISTORIANS AGREE THAT industrial ragu began in the U.S. around 1937. The product was introduced to consumers by Giovanni and Assunta Cantisano. In short order it became Ragù, a trademarked, mass-produced condiment. We owe the Cantisanos a debt of dubious gratitude when we see these products assembled on a grocery store shelf: Ragù Chunky Garden Style Sauce, Ragù Chunky Garlic and Onion Sauce; Ragù Homestyle Thick and Hearty Flavored with Meat Sauce, Homestyle Thick and Hearty Four Cheese Sauce, Homestyle Thick and Hearty Mushroom Sauce, Thick and Hearty Roasted Garlic Sauce, Thick and Hearty Tradi-tional Sauce; Ragù Mushroom Spaghetti Sauce, Ragù Old World Style Traditional Sauce, Ragù Six Cheese Spaghetti Sauce, Ragù Spaghetti Sauce with Meat.

All of them authentic. I think it says so on the jar.

Malcolm Gladwell celebrates the contribution of Howard Moskowitz, a psychophysicist, to ragu in its various current commercial incarnations. Hired by Prego to help the company find out what Americans really wanted from spaghetti sauce to help Prego gain more market share, Moskowitz conducted elaborate nationwide taste tests, accumulating data, and he concluded it was an error to look for one data point, one recipe, a Platonic ideal of ragu that a majority of consumers could agree was the sauce they wanted. Better, Moskowitz advised, to embrace variability. "Sure enough," Gladwell writes, "if you sit down, and you analyze [Moskowitz's] data on spaghetti sauce, you realize that all Americans fall into one of three groups. There are people who like their spaghetti sauce plain; there are people who like their spaghetti sauce spicy; and there are people who like it extra chunky."

IT MAY BE THAT any search for the authentic is doomed because authentic does not really exist. Instead we have variants, iterations that are real-ish.

Go to a trattoria in any town in Emilia Romagna and order lasagna. You will probably be told, "This is the *real* lasagna."

My wife's relatives in Italy argue over whether to include cinnamon (the Spadarolo aunt) or nutmeg (the San Marino aunt) in *passatelli*, an extruded egg-breadcrumb-cheese confection served in broth.

There is vigorous disagreement about whether to put peas in ragu.

In Florence one year, at the Central Market, I had a very satisfying portion of *porchetta*, whole pig seasoned and long-roasted. I told the purveyor I had eaten it before, in San Marino. "That may be," he said. "But this is the *real* porchetta."

When our daughter was old enough to sit at the table and eat pasta, we took her to a local Italian restaurant one night. She ordered spaghetti with ragu. It came to the table served the way pasta is frequently plated in American restaurants, with a very generous dollop of a very red ragu ladled over the top of the pasta. Aghast, she pulled an Alberto. "Not like that!" she cried. My wife plunged a fork and spoon into her dish, mixed the sauce and spaghetti, and our daughter was able, albeit grudgingly, to eat her dinner.

A month ago my wife and I met friends at a trendy new place in Ferndale, one of Detroit's best foody 'burbs. I took a chance and ordered a pasta with heritage pork *sugo*. *Sugo*, I thought. Use of the term sugo (Italian for sauce) seemed to promise something authentic. And it was good. The pasta was cooked just right, the sauce was excellent. Still, when the server set my order in front of me I had an Alberto moment—a deep bowl instead of a shallow one, or better yet a flat dish. Not like that, I wanted to say. Serve long pasta on a flat dish so it can be spread out, rolled on a fork, and eaten the way an Italian would eat it. I wanted to say something. My wife told me to get a grip.

GET A GRIP. THERE'S no such thing as real ragu. There are many ragus, many of them authentic. If Moskowitz were to study it he would find data points: the classical Imola ragus, with chunks of meat, without tomato, with cinnamon or nutmeg; the neoclassical ragus, with ground meat, with tomato, some with peas, some without; and all that stuff in the supermarket that comes in can or jar.

Mario Batali, I notice, has gotten into the business of mass-producing and marketing a variety of sauces. I'm sure he gets them as close as possible to authentic, knowing in his stomach and his soul that no self-respecting Italian would touch them. I'm sure also Jim Harrison wouldn't have gone within ten miles of Mario's sauce in a jar. Not nearly vivid enough for him.

For me either.

# 38

# Bite Down

"WE COULD STOP AND get one on the way back," my wife says. We're lying in bed, both of us awake at three o'clock in the morning.

She's thinking about cake.

In particular about *certosino*, a dense almond-and-pine-nut-and-dark-chocolate cake that's covered with candied fruits and slathered over with honey, a seasonal delicacy you find in Bologna around Christmas time. It's late November. In five days we're flying back to the U.S., but first we're going by train up to Venice for a night, with stopovers in Bologna.

"We could get one on the layover," she says. "Coming home from Venice."

"Let's see," I say, "a layover in Bologna, a cab ride from the train station to Tamburini. It's tempting." But . . .

"Next door to Tamburini," she says. "That bakery."

Bologna is a great food destination we're getting to know. To get to my wife's hometown we fly into Bologna twice a year. We arrive around noon, get into a rental car, and before continuing to San Marino drive into the city for lunch. Always the same route: the Tangenziale, Via Stalingrado, Via del Pallone, Piazza dell'Otto Agosto. We park the car and walk down Via dell'Indipendenza into the old city. In truth it's not all that easy. New Bologna, the periphery, has traffic. You have to *want* to get into old Bologna. Coming home from Venice, even by train, I'm guessing a certosino stop in Bologna will add three hours to our travel time.

I tell her it seems like a lot of trouble to go to for a candy bar.

This remark occasions a pause in our talk, a long lull. I wonder if she has gone back to sleep. Then: "It's not a candy bar," she says. "It's a cake."

In two or three sizes. The small one we'll buy really is the size of a large candy bar. But it's good. Great gods is it good.

While she thinks about cake I lie on my back and ponder a disturbing dream I just had.

"I dreamed I lost all my teeth," I say.

"You love certosino just as much as I do," she says. "Admit it."

"I didn't have any teeth in my mouth. I don't know how I lost them."

"Daddy loved certosino," she says. Her father went to school in Bologna. It's easy to imagine him gorging himself on certosino.

"He had great teeth," I say.

"He had boulders for teeth."

Whereas my father lost all his teeth when I was a kid. I remember him coming home from the hospital toothless; and toothless for a few weeks after that, eating poached eggs for dinner at night, waiting for his dentures to be made.

"If I had to have dentures," I say, "I wonder if they could make me multiple sets. Dentures to wear to the opera, dentures especially designed for eating meat. Dentures to wear to hockey games."

"You hate hockey."

"Dentures for eating *torrone* and *crocante*. Big teeth. Powerful teeth. I could look like that guy."

"Which?"

"That scary guy the kids make fun of. In the movies." We think for a minute. "Gary Busey."

"I don't know him," she says. "Dentures are gross."

In a few minutes her breathing slows. She sleeps while I lie awake imagining a life in which I change my teeth the way I change my clothes.

NEXT DAY ON THE train to Venice I know I'm going to have a problem.

A thin thread of pain runs down my chin. If I lay an index finger on my chin it hurts. What happened was that a few days after we got to Italy I bought a package of dried figs at the grocery store. They came in a box. Inside the box was a hermetically sealed plastic bag, which I raised to my mouth and tore open with my teeth, forgetting I'm not fourteen years old. Something in my mouth went *boink*. There was a subtle but unmistakable popping sensation in that one tooth, a central incisor, bottom row, the tooth with the crown. I knew I had done something.

Yesterday I began to feel mild discomfort. Today I feel it a little more. This is pre-pain. I know what's coming.

I've never had a toothache in Italy.

IN THE SCHEME OF things good teeth must a very recent historical development. Not white teeth, not straight teeth, not cavity-free teeth and the "engineered smiles" modern American dentistry makes possible. I mean just *teeth in your mouth* rather than gaps and holes.

Probably one of the most famous mouthfuls of bad teeth and gaps and holes were those of Queen Elizabeth I. In 1597 Andre Hurault, sieur de Maisse, the French ambassador to Elizabeth's court, observed: "As for her face, it is and appears to be very aged. It is long and thin, and her teeth are very yellow and unequal, compared with what they were formerly, so they say, and on the left side less than on the right. Many of them are missing so that one cannot understand her easily when she speaks quickly." Supposedly she stuffed rags in her cheeks to maintain a fuller face.

You might think, *So that's why she, and every other subject who sat for a painting, never smiled.* It turns out that if you thought that, you would probably be wrong.

During the Renaissance smiling, showing one's teeth, was thought to be bad manners, a breach of etiquette. In fine art you'll find peasants with their mouths open (one of my favorites being Frans Hals's *Laughing Boy*), but individuals with social standing—

people with the inclination and wherewithal to say to a painter, Hey, will you paint my picture?—they kept their mouths shut. Teeth, writes Toby Ferris in "A Brief History of Teeth in Art," are reminders of carnality and death. Caravaggio's *Triumphant Eros* was scandalous in the painter's day because of the boy's smile. Says Ferris: "The damned in last judgments, wedded in life to their mortal flesh, have teeth, and they gnash them. So do all manner of animals and devils. So, of course, do skulls, teeth bared in death. And so, not strangely in all these connections, does the dead Christ."

Everyone else kept their mouths shut in the interest of decorum.

This convention endured for centuries. People in paintings did not smile. Those in photographic portraiture, the same.

Your smiling self is suspicious, creepy, arguably not your real self. Witness the injunction for passport photos: no smiling.

On my phone, about the time the train is passing through Padova, I decide to google home remedies for toothache. I figure it's worth a try.

*Salt water rinse.* Something tells me I'm going to need stronger medicine than that.

*Ice it.* Definitely not going to happen. Unlike Americans Italians are not an ice-loving people. On any given day, in all of Italy there are perhaps two kilos of ice available.

There are other forms of self-help; some of them seem, well, smelly.

Hold a *paper bag soaked in vinegar* to the pained surface. This seems like a desperate act.

*Peppermint oil.* According to Claire of Everyday Roots peppermint oil is "an effective pain blocker." Claire of Everyday Roots reports, "Menthol is a k-opioid receptor agonist," which sounds promising, especially the "opioid" part. *Menta piperita* in Italian. I tell myself to remember that.

*Cloves* are supposed to help. A clove in Italian is referred to as a *chiodo*, which is also the word for *nail*. That sort of puts me off.

*Myrrh* is good for toothache. Maybe it was used on the teething baby Jesus. I look up the word in Italian. *Mirra.*

*Alcohol.* Of course. Soak a cotton ball in whiskey or bourbon. It worked on our babies when they were teething. So that's a possibility.

Five more days in Italy. The idea of having to find a dentist is worrisome—making an appointment, the translation issues, the payment, and follow-up.

I test the tooth with my tongue. It definitely feels busted.

I COULD TAKE COMFORT in the fact that one of the groundbreaking books on teeth was written by an Italian. One Bartolomeo Eustachi, a Renaissance physician and scientist who was avid about dissections and autopsies, published *Libellus de Dentibus* in Venice in 1563. The *Journal of the History of Dentistry* celebrates its "descriptions of the dental pulp, the periodontal membrane, the development of both sets of teeth from dental follicles, the trigeminal nerve, and other oral structures." Between that time and the advent of pain-free and sedation dentistry in the twentieth century, however, the horrors of toothache, and violent relief from it, are colorfully documented, testifying to the arts and entrepreneurialism and humanity of barbers, wigmakers, blacksmiths, shoemakers, and veterinarians. In Carson McCullers's novel *Clock Without Hands* one of her characters reports, "When Doc Tatum died I had a terrible toothache, so I went to Doc's brother who was the best mule doctor in the county."

WE CHECK INTO OUR hotel and walk up the riva to the gardens. We're here for the last days of the Bienialle. It's a damp, foggy day. We walk through twenty or so pavilions, each dedicated to one artist chosen to represent his or her country. Some of the exhibits call to my mind T. S. Eliot's "heap of broken images," challenging art, art that really makes you stretch. Among the memorable exhibits, these: In the Norway pavilion rooms of stacked windows and panes and shattered glass; in the Swiss pavilion a pool of thick, bubbling pink chemical soup; in the Romanian pavilion conventional framed pieces, some of them representational, which I appreciate, among them a few portraits that capture the way I am beginning to feel.

Walking back toward the hotel I hold an aspirin next to the tooth and gum area, letting it dissolve. I'm wondering whether nearby there's a liquor store where I can buy some bourbon, or a *mirra* and *menta piperita* store.

That night we have a mix of fish and shellfish for dinner, also a lot of Prosecco. The chewing is easy. It occurs to me that there will be no need for seafood dentures, unless, of course, I take a great liking to squid.

Wine helps with the pain, sort of.

Next day, late afternoon, I get my dentist in Detroit on the phone. She's thrilled I'm calling her from Italy. She says in forty years of dentistry this is a first for her.

"We're on a train," I say. "Just leaving Venice."

"You're calling from the train?" she says. "Really?" I can hear her telling her assistant, Sara, that my wife and I are calling her from a train in Italy.

I explain the purpose of our trip. Art and food. And Venice at night is great.

She says she's heard of the Bienialle. Wants me to tell her about it when I see her next.

Finally I can come to the purpose of the call. My tooth, the crown, the pain.

I ask her if I should go to a dentist.

"First of all," she says, "stop putting aspirin on that tooth. That's very bad. You're going to burn the gum tissue."

"How about myrrh for pain?" I ask. "Or peppermint oil?"

"What?"

I decide not to mention the bag-soaked-in-vinegar cure. Or the Prosecco.

"By the sound of it," she says, "you need to get going on a course of antibiotics. That's what I would do. That should get you through the next few days."

"Pharmacy," I say to my wife. We're passing Padova.

"Bologna," she says. "*Certosino.*"

I don't have a prescription.

In another thirty minutes we detrain and grab a cab up Via dell'Indipendenza. A couple blocks from Tamburini we tumble out of the cab and into a pharmacy. I get my dentist on the phone again and translate her prescription to the pharmacist, who says, sure, I can get antibiotics over the counter. No prescription necessary. We haggle briefly about dosage (my dentist likes two five-hundred-milligram doses a day, the pharmacist has only thousand-milligram bunker busters).

So I go with the hard stuff.

"While we're here," my wife says.

"Yes."

We rush to the bakery, each of us feeling our sense of elation, and buy two cakes, one for that evening in San Marino, the other for when we get back to the U.S.

"You're going to be okay," she says, more question than assertion.

"I hope I am. I should be," I say. For the time being. I muster an uncertain smile.

# 39

# Difficult Worm

I ASK MY WIFE, "Do you hear that?"

"What?"

In the distance, behind our apartment, there's the whine of truck traffic on the main road on the mountain; closer, two motor scooters accelerate up the street behind us. There's that, but also, softer, somewhere in our building, I hear *ton-ton, ton-ton, ton-ton*.

"Like a phone off the hook," I say, "or an emergency signal."

"I don't hear it." It's after eleven at night. She's getting out of the shower. "It was heaven down there today," she says.

Down the coast in Pesaro this afternoon she went to Marcello and got her hair done. It can take up to three hours for her to move through all the stations of the salon. There must be eight to ten, each with its designated, uniformed, and probably licensed professional. The penultimate stop, before dry and sculpt, is Marcello. He's funny, Italian-guy thin and fashionable. He cuts. But it's the guy who shampoos and massages that my wife loves. He gives her long, luxurious head rubs. She says it went fifteen minutes or so today, maybe longer.

"Heaven."

Another scooter goes up the hill, an older one. The engine sounds hoarse.

"I've been calling him Marco for the past ten years," she says. "I mentioned him at the desk today when I was leaving, they said his name is Rafaello. I apologized to him. 'Why didn't you tell me?' 'Call me Rafaello, call me Marco,' he said. 'Either one is okay.'"

"I could do that for you," I say.

"What?"

"Head massage."

"I don't think so. You don't have the hands."

I hold up my hands, trill my fingers at her.

"I know," she says. "But when I ask you for a neck massage, or a shoulder or back massage, you're too hard, or you can't find the right spots. And after minute or two you get tired. Your heart's not in it."

She's right.

"My heart's not in it," I say. "You're right."

"You see?"

"But head massage, I'd give you both heart and hands."

"No, thank you."

"Both heart and both hands. That's double both."

"It's not like any schmo can do a head massage."

"How hard can it be? I could just watch Marco Rafaello."

"No, thank you."

"I could watch him, then have him give *me* a head massage."

"He's had training. There's technique. There are zones, *areas* that he knows."

"Okay, but let's say he gives me a head massage, visiting all my zones, and I really pay attention. I watch in the mirror. The process sinks in. Then I can give you one."

"You can't watch in the mirror. Your head's wet. It's in the sink."

*Ton-ton, ton-ton.* "You don't hear that?"

She checks out her hair in the mirror, picks up her toothbrush. "He's Neapolitan. All I heard was that *motorino* a minute ago."

Now I can't hear it anymore. Did I really hear it? Should I put it down for auditory hallucination?

Later, in bed, she says, "I think I've read this book already." *Cristo Si E' Fermato a Eboli.*

Since she started reading it she's told me that two or three times.

She waits a few seconds, tells me I should have my hearing checked.

"I heard you, three times. I think you read it in English."

"It's bleak."

"Life is bleak," I say. "Unless it isn't. Head massage, for example."

She shuts off her light, tells me she needs to go up and see Zia tomorrow.

Her old aunt has been in the hospital for a couple weeks now. She's ninety-two. She was weak. She couldn't eat. She had a temperature. She and her caretaker, her *badante*, went up the hill to the hospital, to *pronto soccorso*, their emergency facility. Next thing you know auntie's admitted, and next thing you know next, she's in isolation. She's a regal old girl even in the hospital. Past stays in the hospital she gets up in the morning and puts on her eye make-up, lipstick, the works; wears her plush *vestaglia*, prepares to hold court. This time she's whacked.

"What's wrong with her?" my wife asked the nurse a week ago. Carts rolled up and down the hall. It was dinnertime in the hospital.

"It's something."

"I'm sure it's something," my wife says. "But what? Why is she in isolation?"

"We think it's a kind of worm."

I'm in the hallway listening, working on my medical vocabulary. (Life is bleak. You never know.) "Worm?" I say. I look in at auntie sitting in a chair. Shadows under her eyes, pale blue institutional sickwear. She nods hello in my direction, wags a skeletal digit at me, tells me not to come in.

"She means a bug," my wife says.

"Something in the intestine," the nurse says.

"Virus?" my wife says.

"We're running all the tests. In the meantime, antibiotics."

And isolation. Every visit for the next three or four days my wife ties on the backwards green gown, slips into matching poofy footies, gloves. No mask. Evidently this is not an airborne worm.

Four days go by. The nurse says there are still no results.

"I think they know what it is," my wife says. "They're just not telling us."

Maybe it's the geriatric ward, but, except at mealtime, it seems like they only have half the team on the field in this hospital, unlike in the U.S., where there are crowds of nurses, techs, bloodletters, orderlies, social workers, housekeepers, chaplains, and of course clusters of doctors and predoctors that swarm into rooms to perform detailed oral interrogations and dissections of the patient's condition. In the U.S. the goal is to get you on the entrance ramp to wellness as fast as possible and shove you out the door. Here you are invited to stay. Bring someone with you, invite them to stay too, all day, all night, just in case there is a little ordinary work to be done, like a trip to the bathroom or a walk down the hall.

We see Renzini one day on the floor. He's an affable doctor in a lab coat, there most of the day, available for conference.

"He won't even come in my room," the aunt tells us. "He just stands in the doorway and says, 'Signora, we have to wait for the test results.'"

"What is it?" my wife asks the doctor now.

"Signora, we're not sure yet." Worm, bug, microbe, virus.

Their reticence is the worrisome part. When you get sick over here the diagnosis is often shrouded in mystery. Especially if it's something serious, something likely to kill you, they would prefer not to talk about it.

Odd, because Italians love talking about their health.

Every visit to Italy we make, I stand on the walk in front of our building and talk to Mario. He lives a couple floors above us. He tells me about his most recent medical complaints and the cures he goes for. The cure, as I understand it, is a kind of medical vacation. For a few days you visit a spa, where your ailments are treated with baths and muds, drinks and foods, massages and manipulations. If you're lucky they have a specialist on staff who helps you to find a few new complaints as well; you can stay an extra day or two and head those problems off at the pass.

Then there's Signora Loridana. My wife buys nativity figures from a woman in a Catholic Church accessory store down in Rimini. While I wander around admiring crucifixes and statues of Padre Pio (available in sizes ranging from keychain bob to lifesize), sliding past mannequins modeling priestwear for all ranks and all seasons, Signora Loridana shares her list of afflictions with my wife: bad sleep, headache, stomach ache, sore throat, dizziness, auras, vapors, numbness, twinges. I draw near to listen. One day she says her liver hurts her. She can feel her liver from the *inside* of her body. She has liver ache.

The first line of defense for an Italian is to not get cold.

The scarf is standard equipment, long enough for multiple wraps under the chin. Even well into May everyone wears a jacket and scarf and layer upon layer of long-sleeved shirts and sweaters. The aggregate effect is contained heat and protection from *corrente*. A puff of air can lead precipitously to a stiff neck and who knows what else. *Close that window, shut that door.* I have ridden in cars in August, when it's ninety degrees outside, with the windows shut tight to keep the air outside where it belongs.

No AC. Absolutely not. AC is manufactured *corrente*.

The next time we drive up to the hospital we are finally told something specific. The worm has a name: clostridium. This seems like progress, but we are also told clostridium comes in many different forms. They aren't sure which clostridium it is.

"I think they know," my wife says. "They're just not telling us."

Another week of isolation. Another week of antibiotics.

I do what Americans do: I google clostridium. Its official generic name is *clostridium difficile*. It's a difficult worm. There are indeed hundreds of subvarieties, listed in alphabetical order, among which I note *clostridium asparagiforme* (please don't eat the asparagus), *clostridium cadaveris* (clearly the worst), *clostridium innocuum* (the least terrible), *clostridium putrificum* (ick).

"All those antibiotics," I say to my wife. "The biome in her gut must be wasted."

"What?"

At home I listen to the radio.

"Your gut is a biome, an ecosystem," I say. "Antibiotics are a nuclear option. They kill everything. Zia needs to eat stuff to restore good bacteria in her gut." I consult my medical handbook (Wikipedia) and list good foods for auntie to eat: chicory, garlic, onion, leek, artichoke. Asparagus. (Really?) Italians eat stuff like this. It shouldn't be a problem. Artichokes are in season right now.

"In particularly challenging cases," I say, "fecal transplants have shown promise as a treatment."

I explain about fecal transplants.

"She would never agree to that."

"I think it was Fresh Air I was listening to . . ."

"Forget it," she says. "Never, ever. Ever."

Finally, a few days earlier than we expect, we get the call. They've given auntie her walking papers.

Up at the hospital, while the *badante* helps get auntie dressed, my wife consults with Renzini on what happens next, when auntie should come back for tests, what she should eat, a prescription to be filled. The foods listed in my handbook, he says she shouldn't eat *any* of those.

The four of us ride down the hill, auntie in the front next to me. She's dressed to the nines in God knows how many layers. Vera, the badante, has worked wonders on Auntie's hair. Vera could hold her own next to Marco Rafaello. I keep the windows shut for auntie's benefit even though our black car has been heating up in the sun for two or three hours.

I ask her, "Are you okay, Zia?"

She nods. I swear she's broken a sweat.

I tell her it's a beautiful day.

She nods gravely, says yes, summer seems to have arrived.

In the car it's sweltering.

"Maybe you could put a window down just a little," she says.

Sure, auntie. I really think that would make us all feel a little better.

# 40

# The Enjoy Agenda

A COUPLE SUNDAYS AGO we spent the afternoon in the emergency room in Santarcangelo di Romagna. We went to Santarcangelo because it was a sunny day in April. We went because it's the beginning of pea season. We went because we thought we might shop around a little and then have lunch.

We were in this store and my wife was looking at sweaters and I was trying on a pair of pants in a changing room in the back when I heard her say, Oh.

I peeked out from behind the curtain. Huh?

Oh.

Do these look good on me?

Good, yes.

I was going to wonder out loud, just for fun, Do they make my ass look big? when she steadied herself on a pile of sweaters and said, OH.

What?

I feel dizzy.

I asked her, Do you want to sit down? Of course there was no place to sit down, not even where I was, leaning against the wall in the changing room, struggling in and out of tight Italian pants. I asked her if she ate anything this morning.

You know I didn't.

You don't drink enough water.

I forget.

You're probably dehydrated. Let's get you something to drink.

The Pascucci bar.

Right.

I bought the pants, fast. She leaned and shook her head.

The store guy said, Is signora okay?

We just need to get something to drink, I said. Not, *Oh she'll be all right*, which would have been disrespectful of her plight.

She'll be all right, I thought.

She should be all right, I thought.

Last October I was out strolling one evening with a group I took to Florence, twelve of us total, and I noticed myself listing to the right as I walked. One minute I was perfectly level, the next minute it felt like the edge of the sidewalk had suddenly dropped six inches and I was about to keel over into the street. I didn't say anything. I just kept walking. Oops, lean left. Oops, lean hard left. It went on like this for ten or fifteen minutes. I remember thinking, What should I do? I'll be all right. It was the second day of an eight-day excursion. Next day I was taking people to Lucca. A few days later I was taking people to Venice. Was I going to be seasick on the sidewalk in Venice? Then the dizziness passed. Next morning I got out of bed and sat right back down. What the hell. Then that passed.

It used to be I took people to Italy and worried about one of *them* getting sick. When my wife and I started staying longer I thought about one of us getting sick. I called Blue Cross one day before we left and asked about medical attention, hospitalization, the coverage. Oh, you just put everything on your credit card, they said, and bring the paperwork home with you.

Outside the store that Sunday, fifty feet or so to the right in the main piazza, was our favorite place in town to sit, next to the Tonino Guerra fountain, the Pascucci bar, where just now the Santarcangelini were turned out in their finest duds, having their coffees and their pastries and their cigarettes. My wife suggested we take a seat in the sun. I understood. Fresh air. But smoky fresh.

Some orange juice, please, she told the server.

That'll fix you up, I said.

I sure hope so.

Sir?

I deliberated. It was almost noon. White wine, I guess. I glanced at my wife, borderline optimistic; borderline terrible husband. I shouldn't enjoy myself too much, not yet.

She closed her eyes, faced the sun, and assumed her tanning pose. When it arrived she drank down her orange juice, ordered another with a ham sandwich, which she scarfed, saying *oh damn* a couple times between bites. She drank the second juice down and looked at me.

Maybe we should move into the shade, I said. Aren't you hot?

She shook her head.

Still dizzy?

I thought it would pass.

Me too. I picked up my glass and took a sip. My wine was half gone, still cold.

It should have passed by now, she said.

That's what I thought.

Excuse me, signorina, she said to the server. Can you tell me where the *pronto soccorso* is?

FUNNY. A FEW WEEKS before we left for Italy I talked to a couple pals who get around. They take out insurance when they get around so they can *get back* in case of an emergency. Yeah, Rick, with this policy, if you're admitted to a hospital you just call them. Wherever you are they pick you up and fly you home. They don't just get you home. They deliver you to the hospital of your choice. Well that sounds good, I thought. Then a couple unnerving tales: A business associate vacationing somewhere in the Caribbean with chest pains and no insurance who paid $30,000 to get home fast. A business associate on safari with his family in Africa whose eight-year-old fell down and broke a femur. Righto, stuff happens. Acute brain tumor attack in Florence, for example. Or not. We're at that age, we don't want to stay home. We just need to go away more carefully.

Did I take out insurance?

No.

WE DROVE THREE BLOCKS to the Santarcangelo hospital. She got a gurney in a hallway. She lay back and got her temperature and blood pressure taken, described her symptoms and relevant history (hypoglycemia). It was a busy Sunday in the small emergency room. Forty-year-old male, messed up shoulder. Seventy-year-old male, broken rib. Eighty-year-old female, red rash on her neck and arm. A skinny teenager, coughing. After an hour she was rolled in to have a chat with a doctor. I was not invited.

At the end of the hall was a coffee bar, leave it to the Italians, where I could have an espresso and fizzy water. And wait.

You should go eat, my wife said when she resumed her place in the hall.

No.

Yes, you should go eat. Peas, remember?

Oh yes, I remembered. Peas. But no. No, I said.

I don't know how long I'm going to be here, she said. They took some blood. We have to wait for blood work. Maybe more tests. A heart thingie.

I heard heart thingie and thought, Just put everything on your credit card. Bring the paperwork home with you.

She said, Then I'll have to see the doctor again. It's a gorgeous day and you're just sitting here and I've ruined everything. I've ruined the whole day.

Don't be silly.

She was right though, at least about the gorgeous day, and I was just sitting. Well, standing there.

It feels good to lie back, she said.

We waited ten, fifteen, twenty minutes. I walked over to a front office, which I knew damn well was check-in or triage, where an older man all in hospital whites appeared to be amusing himself on the computer. It took a couple minutes of intensive standing to wrest his attention away from the computer.

What? he said.

Just wondering what's happening, I said. Signora Canducci?

He looked at me like I was a moron. Probably I talked like one, I could give him that. He told me he didn't know, he just got people in the building. Did I want him to get the doctor? The way he asked, it was like, did I want him to jump off the roof.

No, I said. Just checking.

RAVIOLI WITH FRESH PEAS in a light tomato sauce. Stewed rabbit. Swiss chard. A few oven-roasted potatoes. Out of habit I asked for the half-liter of red wine. It's part of the enjoy agenda. Life is short? Still, I was determined to drink only some of it. When Adriana, the proprietor, came by my table, I was mopping up cacciatore sauce with a chunk of bread.

You're by yourself today?

Oh, boy.

Well, I said, Tiziana is over at the hospital right now, in the emergency room. She was feeling light-headed.

Really.

I poured water in the glass next to my wine goblet, emphatically drank some water. Filled in some hospital details. She was feeling way better, I said, when I left.

Ah.

Yup.

I considered trying to say "dehydrated" in Italian. Or "hypoglycemia." Both terms, with all those syllables and treacherous stresses, seemed way out of reach. She needs to drink more water, I said. But she was feeling better when I left. (That's right, I left.) They're checking to make sure nothing's wrong.

How long has she been there?

Oh, a quite a while. We're waiting for results. Blood work. She insisted I come for lunch.

There was still some wine in the carafe.

Insisted I come for lunch, I said.

Dessert?

No, I couldn't possibly. At a time like this?

WHEN I GOT BACK she'd been moved out of the hall and into a room in emergency, with coughing teenager and the old broken rib, who was now coughing a gooey cough all his own. The nurse came to draw her blood again. What is this, I thought, before and after? The blood sample would get driven to a lab in Rimini (five to seven miles away). The results came back by email.

My wife said, They wanted to give me a thing called a TAC. I think it's an MRI.

Oh really.

I refused, she said.

That's probably fine.

This bed came with a chair. With my feet propped up on the rail of her bed I was almost comfortable. On both her wrists and a foot I saw the blue sticky EKG contacts. The kid and broken rib both coughed and coughed.

I feel better, she said.

That's good.

How was lunch?

Ravioli.

With peas?

Adriana asked about you.

What'd you say?

That you made me go for lunch.

WE GET OUT OF there around six that night. The diagnosis is somewhere between inconclusive and nonexistent. In her exit interview they said maybe, just maybe, they saw something in her

EKG. They verify our addresses—the one in the U.S., the one in San Marino— and print copies of all the test results and a summary of the services: six hours in emergency, blood work, EKG, doctor and a couple nurses, technicians, Mr. Personality up front in triage. What'll it cost, I wonder. They say we'll have to come back on a weekday to pay the bill. Billing is down there by the coffee bar.

We have relatives in Canada who go to Florida in the winter. They buy health insurance. The U.S. is notorious. Who can afford to get sick in the U.S.? Over the years, when friends and relatives from Italy have visited us, no one ever has needed medical attention. If there was a toothache or a fever, around home we could call a dentist friend, a doctor friend. But away from home, if someone had to go to the emergency room for six hours, for blood work, EKG, doctor and a couple nurses, technicians, and our own version of Mr. Personality? I shudder to think what it would cost. Thousands of dollars easily.

We wait two weeks before we go back to Santarcangelo. We joke a little with the guy at the pay-your-bill sportello window. He could teach Mr. Personality a thing or two. I slide our papers through the slot along with my credit card.

Okay, he says. And rings up a sixty-euro charge on my card.

I look at my wife. She smiles and shrugs. She's feeling good these days. Six hours and all the rest of it for sixty euros. I feel dizzy, and giddy, and lucky. The cashier staples the credit card receipt to the rest of the papers and slides them over. Paperwork to bring home.

It's a sunny day and the peas are still in season. Adriana will be open for lunch. We'll stop by Pascucci for coffee, *really* have coffee, or maybe a glass of wine. After a little walk around town we'll have lunch and then drive across the hills back home, back to San Marino.

For now the enjoy agenda is in full effect.